Secrets of the Catfish Pros

MINNETONKA, MINNESOTA

Editor Dick Sternberg, a "river rat" at heart, combines his unique biological perspective with his outstanding angling skills to explain catfishing in a way everyone can understand.

Secrets of the Catfish Pros

Printed in 2004.

Tom Carpenter
Creative Director

Gina Germ
Photo Editor

Michele Teigen
Senior Book Development Coordinator

Shari Gross
Laura Belpedio
Book Development Assistants

Glenn Sapir
Research Editor

Brook Martin
Research Assistant

Beowulf Ltd.
Book Design & Production

Principal Photography
Bill Lindner Photography (Bill Lindner, Mike Hehner, Tom Heck, Jason Lund, Pete Cozad)

Additional Photography
In-Fisherman pp.: 11, 14
National Fresh Water Fishing Hall of Fame p.: 12
Roger Aziz pp.: 17, 138
Dick Sternberg pp.: 25, 73, 76-77, 77, 80 all, 84 all
Chris Altman p.: 60 both
Don Wirth p.: 69
Doug Stamm pp.: 79, 81
Minnesota DNR Fisheries Department p.: 81(3)
Brook Martin pp.: 85 both, 106-107, 108, 109, 111 both, 115 all, 116(2), 117 both, 123(2)
Lowrance Electronics p.: 90
Wayne Pinkerton pp.: 93 all, 95 all, 96, 98(2)
Jim Niemiec p.: 99
Keith Sutton pp.: 110, 128
Keith Lambert pp.: 118, 119, 120, 121
Darrell Van Vactor p.: 126
Ed Davis p.: 132
Barry Mullin p.: 136
Tom Carpenter p.: 145

Illustration
Joe Tomelleri pp.: 10, 13, 15, 17, 18, 19, 20
Bill Reynolds pp.: 27, 31, 36 all, 39, 43 both, 49, 53, 56 all, 58 both, 63 both, 80, 83, 87, 88, 91, 94, 103 both, 105 both, 112 both, 113 both, 127, 129, 131, 133, 137, 139
Jeff Atkinson p.: 47

2 3 4 5 / 07 06 05 04
ISBN 1-58159-097-0
© 2001 North American Fishing Club

North American Fishing Club
12301 Whitewater Drive
Minnetonka, MN 55343
www.fishingclub.com

CONTENTS

INTRODUCTION

We call them the *Catfish Pros*.
But these guys—the experts whose catfishing secrets follow—don't fit the usual definition of *fishing pros*. They don't drive the biggest, fastest or fanciest boats on the river or lake. (Heck, some of them don't even *own* a boat!) They don't get featured in the glitzy pages of magazines or on the glorious waters of Saturday morning TV fishing shows. Theirs aren't household names. Most of them don't make much, if any, of their living from catfishing.

But in the end they truly are pros because they each do one thing exceedingly well, probably better than anyone in North America: Catch catfish.

Here are anglers from the North, South, East and West who can help *you* catch more and bigger catfish wherever you live, wherever you fish. Their secrets, strategies, techniques and tips are revealed in the pages that follow, because that's just the way catfish lovers are. We're just regular guys having a good time, catching some fish (maybe even a few eaters for the pan) and, of course, looking for that monster of a lifetime—a freshwater fish that will leave you standing there all weak-kneed and shaking whether you land him or he breaks your rod in half.

No matter what your catfishing goals, *Secrets of the Catfish Pros* will help you get there.

Steve Pennaz

Executive Director
North American Fishing Club

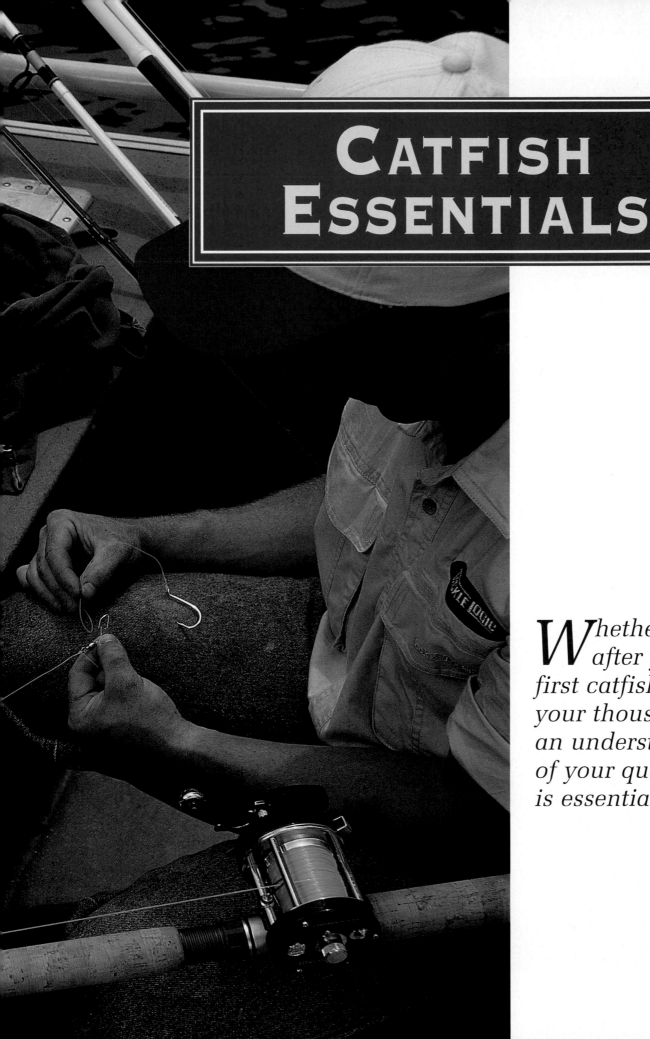

CATFISH ESSENTIALS

*W*hether you're after your first catfish or your thousandth, an understanding of your quarry is essential.

CATFISHING: THE NEW WORLD

Only a decade ago, catfish were the Rodney Dangerfield of freshwater gamefish—they got no respect! In fact, many states didn't even consider them gamefish. They were commercial fish that could be harvested with trapnets, gillnets, seines and practically every other kind of commercial fishing gear.

While that mentality still persists in some states, most natural resource agencies now realize that catfish have more value on the end of a fishing line than in the fish market.

It's not that fishermen have suddenly discovered catfish. In terms of nationwide freshwater angler participation, catfishing has ranked right near the top for decades, along with bass and panfish fishing. But only in the last few years have catfish been held in high esteem by so many anglers. They now receive top billing on TV fishing shows and in national fishing magazines, and anglers can even participate in big-money catfishing tournaments.

There are many reasons why catfish have achieved such a high level of respectability:

•Catfish are widely distributed in the contiguous U.S., and their range is broadening thanks to ambitious stocking programs. The vast majority of American anglers can find some type of catfish within an hour's drive of their home.

•The simplicity of catfishing appeals to many anglers. You don't need a fancy metalflake boat rigged with every

Catch-and-release catfish? Of course! This giant cat may provide the thrill of a lifetime for another angler.

possible kind of electronic gadgetry, you don't need half a dozen tackle boxes filled with every imaginable artificial lure, and you don't need super-sensitive rods made of the latest generation of space-age graphite.

•In many areas, you can catch just as many catfish from the bank as you can from a boat.

•Powerful fighters, catfish wage a determined battle that would put most of the more glamorous gamefish to shame.

•Catfish are ravenous feeders, making them an easy target for anglers.

•With the exception of sturgeon, catfish are the largest freshwater gamefish in North America. On some waters, anglers have a reasonable chance of catching a 50-pound-plus fish.

•Catfish are excellent on the dinner table. They have delicate, white, mild-tasting flesh.

Although catfish are thriving in the majority of waters in which they occur naturally or have been stocked, they still face some serious threats. Where commercial fishing is still legal, catfish often run small and the trophy potential is limited. But commercial fishing may not be the entire problem. In states where the tradition of commercial fishing is still intact, angling limits are usually quite liberal, and fishermen harvest enormous numbers of catfish for food.

To ensure quality catfishing in the future, the "harvest mentality" of some fisheries managers and anglers will have to change. Commercial fishing must be phased out and catfishermen will have to release more of their catch, especially the trophy-sized cats, which may be more than 20 years old.

THE CAST OF CHARACTERS

All North American catfish belong to the family *Ictaluridae,* which means "fish cats." Ictalurids have four pairs of barbels (whiskers); a fleshy adipose fin (small fin on back); smooth, scale-free skin; and bony spines in front of the dorsal and pectoral fins. There are 37 Ictalurid species in North America including channel, blue, flathead and white catfish as well as black, brown and yellow bullheads.

Although these species have a lot in common, there are some significant differences that anglers need to understand.

CHANNEL CATFISH

The channel cat is the most adaptable of North America's big catfish. It is more tolerant of turbidity than its cousins, and can survive in most any unpolluted warmwater environment.

Channel cats thrive in medium- to large-size rivers with slow to moderate current, but they are also found in shallow to mid-depth reservoirs and in small lakes and ponds. Channels will not tolerate as much current as blue cats. They prefer a clean sand, gravel or rubble bottom with an abundance of cover such as logjams, wing dams or brush piles. They're commonly found in tailrace areas where there is an abundance of food.

The native range of the channel catfish extends from the Appalachian Mountains west to the Rockies, and from the Hudson Bay drainage south to the Gulf of Mexico. Their preferred temperature range, 75 to 80°F, is slightly lower than that of flatheads and blues, explaining why their native range extends farther north. Channel cats have been widely stocked in the

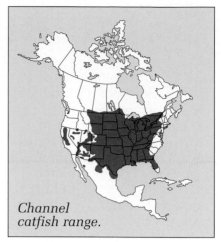

Channel catfish range.

United States, particularly in western reservoirs.

Channel cats spawn in late spring, usually at water temperatures in the 70 to 75°F range. Like other cats, they're difficult to find at spawning time. They build their nests in dark, secluded spots such as holes in the bank, sunken barrels or alongside boulders or logs. Males protect the nest until the young disperse.

During the spawning season, males typically assume a dark blue-black color and

Channel Catfish (Ictalurus punctatus). *Channel cats resemble blue cats; in fact they're often called "blue channel cats." The sides are bluish to greenish gray with a silvery tinge. As channel cats age, they turn a slate blue color, much like that of the blue catfish. Channels can easily be differentiated from blues by examining their anal fin. It is noticeably shorter than that of a blue, with 24 to 29 rays compared to 30 to 36 in a blue. The bottom edge of the anal fin is also more rounded.*

Female channel cats (left) have narrower heads and slimmer shoulders than males (right). Females also have more rounded bodies, while males have a thick, fleshy upper jaw that protrudes well past the lower.

Juvenile channel cats (called fiddlers) and small adults commonly have numerous black spots, which usually disappear as the fish grows older.

their heads become knobby and swollen while the lips thicken and look somewhat fleshy.

Of all the catfish species, channels have the least selective food habits. They will take live fish as well as dead or rotting fish, and will also eat larval aquatic insects, terrestrial insects, crayfish, crabs, snails and clams. Channel cats tend to consume more fish as they grow older, and they reach the largest size in waters where fish make up the bulk of their diet.

Channel cats may feed at any time of the day or night, but veteran catfishermen know that feeding is heaviest after sundown. Channels are also known for their habit of gorging themselves when the water starts to rise.

Channel cats have been known to live more than 20 years, but the usual life span is 10 years or less. In the North, it takes 7 to 9 years for a channel cat to reach 3 pounds. In the South, they reach that size in only 4 or 5 years.

Most channel cats taken by anglers range from 1 to 10 pounds, with 2- to 4-pounders being most common. As is true with most catfish, male and female channel cats grow to roughly the same size.

Willing biters, channel cats respond to "stinkbaits" better than flatheads or blues. They can also be attracted by chumming, usually with rotten cheese or fermented grain. In addition, channels can be taken on dried blood, chicken liver, worms, minnows and even artificial lures such as jigs and spinners.

The all-tackle, world-record channel cat is W. B. Whaley's 58-pound giant taken from South Carolina's Santee-Cooper Reservoir system on July 7, 1964.

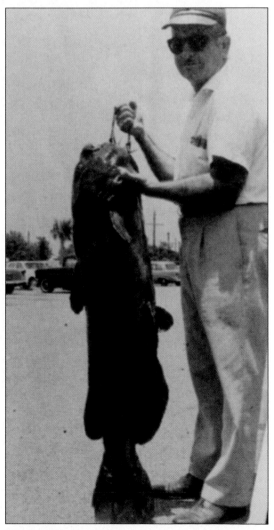

W. B. Whaley and his world-record channel cat.

Ken Paulie and his world-record flathead.

FLATHEAD CATFISH

With the official recognition of Ken Paulie's 123-pound flathead, caught in Elk City Reservoir, Kansas, in 1998, the flathead can now be called North America's largest catfish species.

Also known as the mud cat, yellow cat, Appaloosa cat, shovelhead cat and Johnnie cat, the flathead inhabits large river systems, including any impoundments and major tributaries.

Despite the name mud cat, flatheads seldom frequent areas with a soft bottom. River-dwelling flatheads spend most of their time in large, sluggish pools with a sandy or gravelly bottom or in the food-rich tailwaters of dams. In impoundments,

you'll often find flatheads around flooded timber, stumps or tangles of woody cover.

Flatheads prefer water temperatures in the upper 70s to low 80s and can tolerate temperatures of more than 90°F. Contrary to popular belief, they are not able to survive in highly polluted waters or in waters with extremely low dissolved oxygen levels.

In the North, flatheads begin moving into traditional wintering holes in late fall. Thousands of cats congregate in a few acres of water, usually where there is an abundance of rocky or woody cover to break the current. They spend the winter in a state of near dormancy, lying flat to the bottom and allowing a layer of silt to accumulate on their back. They remain in these wintering holes until the water begins to warm in spring.

An extremely efficient predator, the flathead has broad, powerful jaws with a large pad of tiny recurved teeth on the upper jaw that makes it virtually impossible for prey to escape once the fish clamps down on it.

Flatheads have been observed holding quietly on

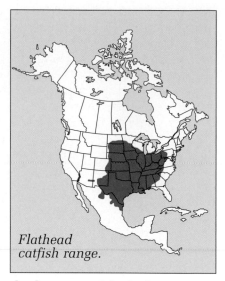

Flathead catfish range.

the bottom with their enormous mouths opened wide, waiting for a smaller, hapless fish to investigate the curious cavity.

The flathead's diet consists mainly of live fish but flatheads also eat crayfish and clams. Unlike channel catfish, flatheads rarely consume rotten food. This explains why fishermen use fresh, lively baitfish such as suckers, carp, large shiners and sunfish, or fresh cut bait, rather than the "stinkbaits" and other prepared baits that work so well for channel cats. It's not unusual for an angler pursuing big flatheads to bait up with a 2-pound carp or sucker.

Secretive, solitary fish, flatheads feed mainly at night, moving from the security of woody cover in a deep pool to forage in a shallow riffle area. After feeding, an adult flathead returns to its favorite resting spot where it remains until the next night, unless it is disturbed. So it's easy to see why the best flathead anglers are night stalkers.

Flatheads spawn in late spring or early summer, a little later than channel cats. Spawning usually takes place at water temperatures in the low to upper 70s. The fish often spawn in a natural hole in the bank, but they may excavate nests near logs or boulders. "Noodlers" take advantage of the flathead's spawning habits by reaching into holes in the bank and grabbing fish that may exceed 70 pounds. Many noodlers have missing fingers that demonstrate the power of the flathead's jaws.

It's not unusual for flatheads to live 15 years, and some individuals probably live much longer. In the North, a 15-year-old flathead averages about 30 pounds; in the South, more than 50.

Five- to 10-pound flatheads are most commonly caught by anglers, and 30- to 40-pound fish rarely warrant a mention in a hometown newspaper.

One of the strongest fighting freshwater fish, flatheads typically wage a dogged battle in deep water. You struggle for ten minutes to pull the fish up a few feet, then it retreats to the bottom and you start all over. It's not surpris-

Flatheads have a penchant for eating fish of a size that most anglers would be happy to catch.

ing that serious mudcatters use pool-cue rods and 50-pound line. In much of the South, jug fishing, trotlining and noodling account for

more flatheads than does rod-and-reel fishing.

Flatheads taken from clean water have firm, flaky, white meat with an excellent flavor.

Flathead Catfish (Pylodictis olivaris). *As its name suggests, the flathead has a broad, flattened forehead. The back and sides are usually light brown with darker brown or black mottling, but the coloration varies greatly. Some fish are nearly black while others have a bright yellowish hue. The belly ranges from pale yellow to creamy white. The flathead is the only North American catfish species with a squarish tail and protruding lower jaw; the other catfish have forked tails and underslung lower jaws.*

BLUE CATFISH

Blue cats are capable of growing to even larger sizes than flatheads. In the mid-1800s, commercial fishermen along the Mississippi River caught and butchered blue catfish weighing up to 200 pounds, and a brute tipping the scales at 315 pounds was reportedly caught on the Missouri River in 1866. No blues approaching those sizes have been caught in modern times, but several 100-plus pounders have recently been taken on hook and line. The current world record, a 111-pound behemoth, was caught by William P. McKinley in Wheeler Reservoir, Alabama, in 1996.

Blue cats are big-river fish, thriving in mainstem rivers and their major tributaries. They favor faster, clearer water than channel cats and are usually found over a clean sand, gravel or rubble bottom. They prefer water temperatures in the 77 to 82°F range, slightly higher than the range of channel cats. Like channels, blues are often found in tailrace areas, where food is abundant.

Blue catfish are native to the Mississippi, Missouri and Ohio river drainages in the central and southern states, and their range extends south into Mexico and northern Guatemala. Blues have been stocked in many reservoirs in both the eastern and western U.S., where they commonly grow to enormous sizes. In some impoundments, however, biologists believe that these fish fail to reproduce.

Blues tend to be more pelagic (open-water oriented) than other cats. They roam widely, often in large

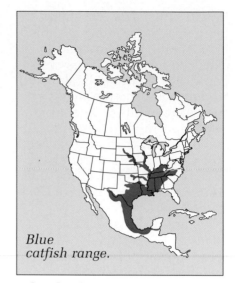

Blue catfish range.

schools, foraging at any depth. Many commercial anglers report catching more blues on trotlines that are suspended under the surface than on those fished on the bottom.

Biologists consider blue cats "opportunistic" feeders, because they will eat whatever food is available. Although fish are the primary food of adult blues, they will also take insects, crayfish and clams. Large blues do not hesitate to swallow fish weighing several pounds. In many southern reservoirs and rivers, the diet of blue catfish consists almost entirely of gizzard and threadfin shad.

Blue cats feed at any time of the day or night and, unlike flatheads, they continue to feed heavily even when water temperatures dip into the 40s.

Blues are more migratory than other catfish species. During the pre-spawn period, they often migrate upriver, congregating in enormous schools below dams that block their spawning run. But as winter approaches, they generally move downriver.

Spawning takes place in late spring or early summer, usually at water temperatures from 70 to 75°F. Blues, like

Given time, blue cats can grow very big. You could even say huge.

Blue Catfish (Ictalurus furcatus). *These fish are bluish to grayish in color, although some are silvery, accounting for the name "silver cat." Blues are stockier than channels, and a blue's head is smaller compared to the rest of its body. The profile, from the dorsal fin forward, is straight and steeply sloped, giving the body a distinctive, wedge-shaped appearance. Like channels, blues have a deeply forked tail, but their sides are not spotted (even on small fish), and their anal fin is much longer (30 to 36 rays), with a straighter bottom edge.*

flatheads and channels, nest in some type of cavity that provides shade and protection from predators. Common spawning sites include undercut banks, root wads, depressions in the bottom and sheltered areas behind boulders.

The life span of a blue is longer than that of other North American catfish; the largest specimens are usually more than 20 years old. Growth varies greatly in different bodies of water, depending on forage availability. In the Louisiana Delta, for example, blues grow to 33.4 inches (about 17 pounds) in only 6 years. In Lake Chickamauga, Tennessee, they reach only 1.2 pounds in the same amount of time.

Blues will take a variety of live baits, cut baits and prepared baits. In addition to hook-and-line fishing, blues are commonly taken by jug fishing, trotlining and noodling.

Considered excellent eating, blues have white, flaky, mild-tasting meat.

Unfortunately, America's blue catfish population has declined since 1900. Dam and lock construction along big rivers has blocked spawning runs, limiting the numbers of blues in many sections of the larger rivers. And by impounding the water, dams take away the current that blues prefer.

Commercial fishing has also taken its toll on the largest blues. Some states are now taking steps to reduce commercial harvest so that more trophy blues are available to sport fishermen.

Small catfish predominate in water with a heavy commercial harvest.

WHITE CATFISH

Because of their smaller size and limited distribution, white catfish are much less popular than the "big three." And where they coexist with channel cats, anglers often fail to make the distinction because the two look so much alike. But white catfish are gaining in popularity as stocking expands their range.

White catfish feed heavily during the daytime, a huge factor in their popularity among anglers east and west.

They are especially popular in "fee-fishing" ponds.

White catfish are commonly found in sluggish streams, marshes, bayous, river back-waters, ponds and reservoirs. Compared to other catfish species, whites are more tolerant of a soft, silty bottom and high water temperatures. Their preferred temperature range is 80 to 85°F. White cats can also tolerate more salinity than other catfish species, so they are often found in the lower reaches of coastal rivers, where other cats are absent.

The white catfish is sometimes called the "Potomac cat," because it was once limited to the Atlantic coastal states—from Chesapeake Bay to Florida—and a few of the gulf states. But whites have been successfully introduced into many waters in California and Nevada, as well as into numerous fee-fishing lakes across the country.

Gluttonous feeders, white catfish prefer small fish but will also take fish eggs, aquatic insects, crustaceans and even pondweeds. Although white cats may feed at night, they are not as nocturnal as the other catfish species.

Like other catfish, white cats spawn in late spring or early summer, generally at water temperatures in the 70 to 75°F range. They build a large nest, usually on a sandbar, and the male guards the eggs and fry.

White catfish may live up to 14 years, but their growth rate is the slowest of all the catfish species. In the northern part of their range, it takes from 9 to 11 years for a white cat to reach 2 pounds. In the southern part, they normally reach that size in 6 or 7 years. The majority of

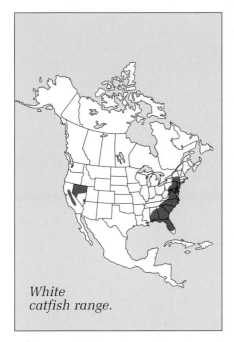

White catfish range.

Although they don't grow to the behemoth sizes of their cousins, white catfish can still reach respectable proportions. This good one is from a Massachusetts tidewater.

white cats caught by anglers weigh from 1 to 3 pounds.

The white cat's willingness to take most any kind of bait, combined with its tendency toward daytime feeding, explains why it is so popular in fee-fishing lakes and ponds.

Whites are scrappy fighters, but their relatively small size limits their popularity in regions where anglers have access to bigger cats.

An excellent table fish, the white catfish has firm, white flesh.

The world-record white catfish, a 22-pounder, was caught on March 21, 1994, by James Robinson in William Land Park Pond, California.

White Catfish (Ameiurus catus). *White cats resemble channels, but do not grow nearly as large. Whites often have the greenish or bluish silver coloration of the channel cat, but there is usually a sharper demarcation between the darker color of the sides and the whitish belly. Some whites are mottled with milky, pale gray to dark blue splotches. The tail of a white is not quite as deeply forked, the body is never spotted, the anal fin is shorter (19 to 23 rays), and the chin barbels are white rather than black or brown.*

Black bullheads thrive in turbid water.

BLACK BULLHEAD

The most common bullhead species, blacks are often so abundant that they become stunted. Where stunting is not a problem, however, they grow to respectable size. In fact, the world record for the black bullhead is larger than that of any other bullhead species.

Often the dominant species in freeze-out lakes, black bullheads can tolerate dissolved-oxygen levels lower than any other freshwater gamefish, with the possible exception of the yellow bullhead (p. 20). Black bullheads are most abundant in lakes and streams with turbid water, a muddy bottom and very little current. They favor water temperatures in the 75 to 85°F range.

Black bullheads spawn in late spring or early summer at water temperatures in the upper 60s. The female builds a nest in weedy or woody cover and, after spawning, she helps the male guard the eggs and young. After the young leave the nest, they can often be seen swimming along the shoreline in tight schools.

The diet consists of a wide variety of foods including small fish, fish eggs, worms, leeches, mollusks, insects and plant material.

Although black bullheads live up to 10 years, their growth rate is highly variable, depending on whether or not the population is stunted. If stunting is not a problem, a black bullhead in the North usually reaches a weight of 1 pound in 7 to 9 years; in the South, only 4 or 5 years.

Black bullheads are not fussy; you can catch them on most any bait including worms, cheesebait, stinkbait liver and even chunks of soap.

Even though black bullheads are weak fighters, their tasty white meat makes them popular with many anglers.

The world-record black bullhead, an 8-pound, 15-ouncer, was caught by Charles M. Taylor in Sturgis Pond, Michigan, on July 19, 1987.

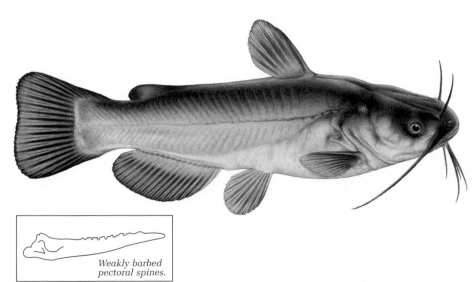

Weakly barbed pectoral spines.

Black bullhead range.

Black Bullhead (Ameiurus melas). *Black bullheads have dark greenish to goldish sides and dark-colored barbels. They are sometimes confused with brown bullheads, but the tail is slightly notched, there is a pale, crescent-shaped bar at the base of the tail and a black's pectoral spines are not as strongly barbed (inset).*

BROWN BULLHEAD

Brown bullheads are usually found in larger, deeper lakes than other bullhead species. They also thrive in some smaller lakes and ponds, and in slow-moving streams, but they are not as resistant to freeze-out as black bullheads. Brown bullheads favor water temperatures in the upper 70s or low 80s.

Spawning takes place in late spring or early summer, generally at water temperatures in the low 70s. Both parents build a nest on a mud or sand bottom, usually among roots, logs or other cover that provides shade. After spawning, they continue to guard the nest and protect the young.

The diet of a brown bullhead is similar to that of a black, consisting of small fish, fish eggs, worms, leeches, mollusks, crayfish, insects and plant material.

Brown bullheads may live up to 12 years, but the usual life span is much shorter. In the northern part of the range, it takes 7 or 8 years to grow a 1-pounder; in the southern part, only 4 or 5 years.

Good-sized lakes produce good-sized brown bullheads.

Although brown bullheads are not strong fighters, they'll give you a little more tussle than a black. Their meat is reddish or pinkish, rather than white, but it is quite firm and has a good flavor.

The world-record brown bullhead weighed 6 pounds, 2 ounces. It was caught by Bobby L. Gibson Jr., in the Pearl River, Mississippi, on January 19, 1991.

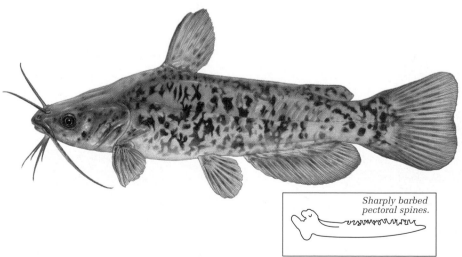

Sharply barbed pectoral spines.

Brown bullhead range.

Brown Bullhead (Ameiurus nebulosus). *Brown bullheads usually have mottled sides and a tail that is square or has only a very slight notch. The pectoral spines (inset) are longer and more sharply barbed than those of a black bullhead and there is no pale crescent-shaped mark at the base of the tail.*

YELLOW BULLHEAD

Although bullheads are usually considered a muddy-water fish, yellow bullheads prefer clear water with a heavy growth of aquatic vegetation. But they can tolerate polluted water and extremely low dissolved oxygen levels.

Yellow bullheads thrive in warm, slow-moving streams; ponds; small, weedy lakes; and weedy bays of larger lakes. Their preferred temperature range is 75 to 80°F.

The yellow bullhead's diet is not much different from that of other bullheads, but yellows are known for their habit of scavenging most any kind of organic matter off the bottom. They will eat bits of weeds, aquatic insects and other invertebrates and, on occasion, live fish.

Spawning takes place in late spring or early summer, when the water temperature warms to the upper 60s or low 70s. The fish may nest in a cavity in the bank or dig out a depression in a clean bottom. When spawning has been completed, the male guards the nest until the eggs hatch and the fry disperse. Yellows have a lower reproductive rate than blacks, meaning that they're less prone to stunting.

Yellow bullheads grow more rapidly than blacks or browns, but their life span seldom exceeds 7 years. There is little difference in growth rate from north to south. It takes about 5 years to grow a 1-pounder in the northern part of the range and about 4 years in the southern part.

Although yellow bullheads do not put up a strong fight, they are willing biters and, when taken from cool water, are good eating. Effective baits include worms, leeches, crickets, grubs, cut bait, doughballs, stinkbait and cheesebait.

Yellow bullheads abound in clear, weedy lakes.

The largest yellow bullhead on record weighed 4 pounds, 8 ounces. It was caught by Patricia Simmon in Mormon Lake, Arizona, on July 15, 1989.

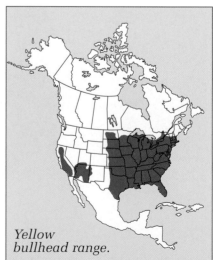

Yellow bullhead range.

Yellow Bullhead (Ameiurus natalis). *Yellow bullheads are easy to distinguish from the other major bullhead species in that they have a rounded tail and light-colored chin barbels. The upper barbels are brown.*

Important Catfish Facts

	Channel Catfish	Flathead Catfish	Blue Catfish	White Catfish
Current Tolerance	Very adaptable; prefers slow current but may feed in riffle areas.	Prefers very light current or no current at all, but may be found in areas of moderate current if there is adequate cover to provide a current break.	Will tolerate more current than any of the other catfish species and may be found in areas of heavy flow in tailwaters and open river stretches.	Prefers little or no current and will tolerate a silty bottom. It is found primarily in lakes, ponds and slow-moving rivers and streams.
Cover Preferences	Often found among or along outside edges of rocky or woody cover, but may roam sandy or gravelly flats with little if any cover.	Very cover-oriented; usually found among sunken trees, brush piles or rocks, or inside hollow objects such as logs and barrels.	Least cover-oriented of all the catfish species; spends much of its time in pursuit of baitfish suspended in open water.	Commonly found around weedy or woody cover in shallow lakes and ponds, river backwaters and slow-moving stream reaches.
Food/Feeding Habits	Versatile feeders, channels cats will eat insects, crustaceans, mussels and live, dead or rotting fish. Channel cats may feed around the clock, but feeding usually peaks just after sunset. Rising water also triggers a feeding binge.	Flatheads prefer live fish but will take fresh, dead ones as well. But unlike channel cats, they will seldom eat rotting baitfish. Other flathead favorites include crustaceans and mussels. Primarily night feeders, flatheads move out of heavy cover after sunset to feed on shallow flats and shoals.	Like channel cats, blues eat a wide variety of foods including insects, crustaceans and mussels, but live fish are the mainstay. Blues don't hesitate to feed in cool water (below 50°F) and can be caught during daylight hours or after dark.	Primarily daytime feeders, white catfish will feed at night as well. They eat small fish and eat just about any other kind of food they can find including insects, crustaceans and even aquatic vegetation.
Best Baits	It's not unusual for anglers tossing jigs, spinners or even crankbaits to catch channel cats, but the majority are taken on worms, minnows, cut bait, shrimp, chicken liver, bloodbait, stinkbaits, and insect baits such as grasshoppers and catalpa worms.	Live baitfish, preferably large, active ones, make the best flathead bait. Fresh cut bait and gobs of nightcrawlers will also catch flatheads, but the fish rarely take stinkbaits or other prepared baits.	Blues, like channels, will take a variety of baits including large, lively baitfish and chunks of cut bait, preferably from a species occurring naturally in the body of water you're fishing. Blues can be taken on nightcrawlers, catalpa worms, shrimp, bloodbaits, liver and prepared baits.	Known as cooperative biters, white catfish are caught on every imaginable kind of catfish bait from worms, minnows and insect baits to liver and stinkbaits.

PROVEN METHODS

*E*ven though you may be familiar with these widely used methods, you may not be up to speed on the finer points that will put more cats in your boat.

OXBOW CATS

by Keith Sutton

If you're a serious catfish angler who likes to fish big rivers, chances are you've explored every nook and cranny of every good-sized waterway in your neck of the woods. And you probably know right where to find the fish at different times of the year and at different water stages.

The problem is, you're not the only one who has all this figured out, so your favorite river-fishing holes probably get "hammered" a lot more than you would like.

During your explorations you may have noticed some backwater lakes that did not appear to be connected to the river. More than likely, you chose to ignore them because there was no way for catfish to get in or out.

That was a mistake! Many of these floodplain lakes, called "oxbows," provide catfishing opportunities as good as—or better than—the main river itself. And for every oxbow lake that you saw when doing your research, there were probably two or three more hidden from your view.

UNDERSTANDING OXBOWS

Scattered like emeralds from a broken necklace, oxbows can be found along almost any good-sized river with a wide, low-gradient floodplain. The best known oxbows, such as Lake Chicot (5,300 acres) in southeast Arkansas, are associated with the Mississippi or other main-stem rivers, but you'll find thousands of smaller oxbows, some covering only a few acres, along warmwater rivers throughout much of the country. These small oxbows are the real jewels because they see practically no fishing pressure. It's not uncommon to fish for a day, or even a week, on a little backcountry oxbow and never see another boat.

Named for the "U"-shaped device used to collar oxen to their yoke, oxbow lakes are also U-shaped and often carry names like "Horseshoe," "Crescent" or "Half-Moon" Lake. Oxbows are sometimes called "cutoffs" or "river lakes."

In any low-gradient river that flows over loose materials, the outside bends are constantly being eroded and silt is deposited in the inside bends. Over time, the snake-like pattern continues to widen, forming loops that turn back on themselves. When two adjacent loops get too close, the neck washes out, forming a new channel and leaving one of the loops isolated from the main river channel. In some cases, the downstream end of the new lake may remain connected to the river.

This process usually occurs naturally but, in some cases, man speeds it up by excavating a new channel so flood-waters can pass downriver more quickly.

Although blues and flatheads frequently inhabit oxbows, channel cats are the bread-and-butter fish of these lakes in most regions. Extremely dense populations may be present, particularly in older oxbows where lots of hollow trees have toppled and created prime spawning holes.

How Oxbows Are Formed

When a river channel forms a sharp loop, flood waters often cut across the neck, forming a new river channel and leaving the old one isolated. The old channel, called an "oxbow" may remain connected to the new channel during periods of high water, or it may become separated so far by subsequent channel changes that no connection is possible.

TYPES OF OXBOWS

A quick glance at a river chart may reveal dozens of oxbows, but not all of them have good catfish potential. Before planning an oxbow adventure, it's important to understand what types of oxbows are most likely to produce under a given set of conditions.

Floodplain Oxbows

Oxbows lying within the river floodplain normally provide the best catfishing. At flood stage, catfish from the main river swim into oxbows and other backwaters to escape the furious current in the main channel and, when the water recedes, they're trapped until the next flood.

Even if the oxbow remains connected to the river at normal stage, the fish often stay put to feast upon the abundant supply of baitfish, crayfish and other catfish delicacies that oxbows normally support.

Isolated Oxbows

Some oxbows lie outside the river floodplain, isolated by levees or dams. Fishing in these oxbows is more predictable than in floodplain oxbows because anglers don't have to contend with such drastic changes in water level.

But without a connection to the main river, isolated oxbows may not hold any catfish and even if they do, the fish are usually small. On occasion, however, you'll find an isolated oxbow with astounding numbers of "eating-sized" cats.

Remember that these are only general guidelines. A few isolated oxbows, for example, offer tremendous fishing for trophy-class cats, and some floodplain lakes have no cats at all. That's why it's important to do your homework before striking out on an oxbow adventure.

Most of the major oxbows along big-river systems have been surveyed, and information on the fish population is available from state fisheries agencies. You may be able to get information on smaller oxbows by inquiring at a bait shop or talking with knowledgeable local anglers.

Another option: Study a river chart or other detailed map to locate little-known oxbows and then carry a small boat overland from the river to check it out. You might be rewarded with an untapped catfish bonanza.

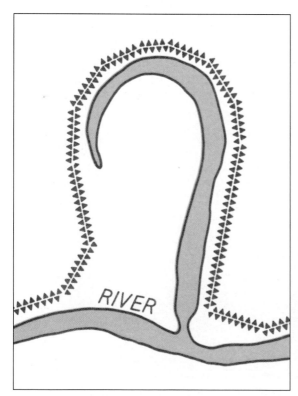

Floodplain Oxbow. This type of lake rises and falls along with the main river, and lies within the river's levee system (zigzag line).

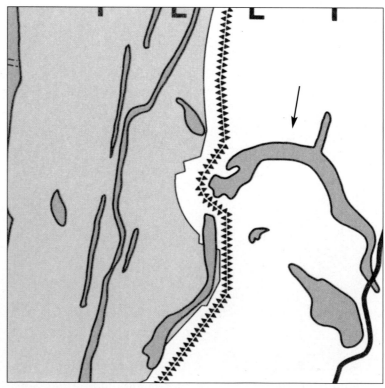

Isolated Oxbow. Because this type of lake (arrow) is separated from the main river by a levee, fish do not have free access to the river unless floodwaters top the barrier.

FINDING OXBOW CATS

Finding oxbow catfish is suprisingly easy because most of these lakes have similar shape and structure.

Oxbows tend to be relatively flat with a fairly uniform depth, but the outside bend of the lake is almost always deeper than the inside bend.

Basic Rules

Here's the general locational pattern that applies in the majority of oxbows: In spring and early summer, you'll find the most catfish scattered among timber, logs and other woody cover along the inside bend. But during the hottest part of the summer and in winter, cats tend to concentrate along the outside bend. There normally is very little deep water, so you don't have to look far to find fish.

In oxbows that remain connected to the main river, you'll want to pay special attention to the outlet channel, which is usually on the downstream end of the lake. Sometimes called the "run-out" or "run-out chute," this channel is a catfish magnet, especially in late spring or early summer when water levels are receding following a spring flood. In most cases, there is only one run-out, but there could be several.

There's a simple reason why run-outs are so productive: They are the only part of the lake with any significant current. When the entire flow of an oxbow is funneled through the narrow chute, current velocity increases dramatically and catfish move into the channel, often in great numbers, to partake of the easy meal carried to them by the moving water. Some of the fish hold near cover at the upstream end of the run-out; others hold in the downstream tail, where the rushing water meets the main river channel.

Timing is the key to fishing a run-out. You can catch some catfish in a run-out any time there is a noticeable current. But fishing is usually best on the few days before the water level subsides to the point where there is no current.

Species Specifics

You may have to modify your basic strategy for finding cats depending on what species are present. For example, blue cats often follow schools of shad and other forage fish, so you'll often find them suspended in open water. In this situation, you'll have to hunt them down with your depth finder. When you see a narrow band of baitfish, chances are you'll find blues right below them.

Oxbow flatheads tend to hole up in dense woody cover. During the spawning season, flatheads are particularly fond of the big dark cavities at the base of huge hollow cypress trees. Other prime flathead spots include big log-jams often found in the run-out chutes, clusters of cypress "knees," buckbrush or willow thickets in shallow water, and shorelines covered with big rock riprap.

Look for channel cats around fallen trees, stump fields, beaver lodges, weedbeds, shoreline riprap and man-made structures such as docks, duck blinds and fish attractors.

Outer bank, deepest water

Run-out

Because oxbows are former river channels, the outside bend almost always has the deepest water. When the oxbow was part of the river, current cut into the outer bank and formed a deeper channel while silt was deposited on the opposite side; this explains why the water there is still shallow. In many cases, a deep channel forms at the downstream end of the lake, called the run-out.

Watch Water Levels

Floodplain oxbows can be tricky to fish because of the extreme water-level fluctuations. When the river rises, the lake rises. When the river falls, the lake falls. Changing conditions dramatically affect catfish location, explaining why serious anglers monitor water levels closely.

As a rule, fishing in floodplain oxbows is best when the water level is steady or slowly rising or falling. The fish don't move much under these conditions, so you can find them in their usual haunts.

When the water rises rapidly, however, catfish start moving and become quite nomadic. A spot that produces one day may not yield a single fish the next day, and vice versa. And to further complicate matters, the cats usually scatter rather than relate to a specific cover.

To help determine what the fish are doing on a particular day, it's important to know the precise water stage at

Common Types of Catfish Habitat in Oxbow Lakes

The run-out chute draws catfish when the water level is receding after a spring flood.

Man-made structures like docks, swimming platforms, duck blinds and submerged fish attractors make good catfish cover.

Cavities beneath large cypress trees, along with the "knees" surrounding the trees, are prime locations for flatheads.

which the main river will overflow into a given oxbow. You'll find water-level gauges at intervals along the course of most major rivers, and those gauges provide the information you need.

Through experience, you'll learn what water level is necessary for the river to start flowing into various oxbows.

Be sure to jot these numbers down and keep them for future reference.

By monitoring the water-level gauges or checking them in your local newspaper, you'll know not only when the river and a certain oxbow are connected, but whether the water is rising or falling and how fast.

Water-level gauge.

Flooded shallow-water brush will attract oxbow flatheads.

The cover provided by fallen trees will attract catfish, especially channels.

Riprap shorelines, especially those along an oxbow's deep outside bend, are good spots for flatheads and channels.

A small jon boat makes an ideal rig for fishing an oxbow. It's light enough for two anglers to portage, if necessary, yet stable enough for them to fish safely on these small and usually calm waters.

FISHING FOR OXBOW CATS

With a few exceptions, fishing for catfish in an oxbow is not much different than fishing for them in any other kind of lake. The exact method, rig and choice of bait depends on the structure and cover you're fishing and the species of catfish you're pursuing.

But oxbow anglers have discovered a few tricks that help tip the odds in their favor when fishing specific kinds of oxbow habitat.

To catch catfish concentrated in run-outs, for example, rig up a slip-float setup with live bait or cut bait, and drift it through the run-out chute. Be sure to adjust the float to keep the bait just off the bottom. Focus on the head and tail end of the run-out.

To extract flatheads from a logjam in the chute, anchor upcurrent from it and drift a live sunfish on a lightly weighted slip-float rig into the tangle (opposite).

When rising water floods the woodlands surrounding oxbows, catfish move out into the maze of timber to feed on a new food source: terrestrial crayfish. These crustaceans are extremely abundant in many bottomland hardwood forests, but during most of the year their terrestrial habits make them totally inaccessible to catfish.

But once their burrows are flooded and the craws begin moving around, they make easy prey for foraging catfish of all species.

The problem is, a rise in water level of only a few inches can flood thousands of additional acres of bottomland, so it's hard to know exactly where to find the fish. And even if you know where they are, you'll have a hard time catching them with rod and reel because of all the snaggy cover.

Savvy catmen solve the problem by using "absentee" methods like trotlining, limblining and yo-yoing.

Tips for Catching Oxbow Cats

To catch catfish buried in a log jam or the "hollows" between the knees of a cypress tree, anchor upwind or upcurrent, rig up a slip-float rig with a very light weight and a sunfish for bait, and let the rig drift right into the woody cover.

With the light weight, a lively sunfish will attempt to swim as far back into the cover as it can, right into the cats' hiding spot.

To make a limbline set when you can't find a springy limb, tie a piece of inner-tube to the line to act as a shock absorber. This makes it more difficult for a hooked catfish to pull free.

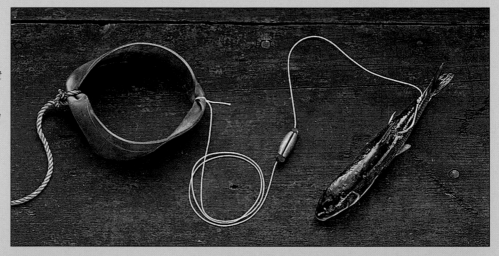

Place yo-yo rigs on limbs (where legal) and check them the next day. These spring-loaded devices set the hook automatically and are popular in much of the South.

Fish an inaccessible oxbow by using a belly boat and kick fins. Some anglers equip these rigs with a depth finder, a small anchor and even a rod holder.

OPEN-WATER BLUES

by Paul Canada

THE DISCOVERY

It's never easy to locate catfish in a huge body of water, and the challenge is even greater when you're looking for giant blues in a sprawling man-made lake.

Blues are the nomads of the catfish clan. Their habit of following schools of baitfish in open water means that they're literally here today and gone tomorrow.

But anglers who understand the open-water nature of big blues have made great strides in piecing together the locational puzzle and developing techniques for putting these elusive eating-machines in the boat.

The first anglers to crack the blue's code were striper guides on large southern impoundments. While fishing giant stripers under schools of open-water shad, these fishermen noticed that they were catching an inordinate number of trophy-class blues by accident.

Randy Dorman, an accomplished bass and striper guide, is also one of the most popular catfish guides on South Carolina's Santee-Cooper impoundments. He believes that blue cat location and activity corresponds with the seasonal movements of large schools of shad. Blues stay close to the food source. So if you find the shad, you'll find the cats.

Randall Hall, who probes the depths of Texoma on the Texas-Oklahoma border, has independently discovered the same pattern. Although the two lakes differ considerably in character, with Lake Texoma being deeper and more highly structured than the Santee-Cooper lakes, the movements of shad determine where you'll find the blues.

Even though the bodies of water that the two men fish are nearly 1,000 miles apart, the techniques they use to find and catch giant blues are remarkably similar.

Randy Dorman with a shad-gulping Santee-Cooper blue.

Find the baitfish and you'll find reservoir blues.

FINDING RESERVOIR BLUES

Throughout most of the year, reservoir blues relate primarily to open water, although some of them slip into coves and tributaries during the spawning period. Here are some tips for following the seasonal movements of reservoir blues.

Winter Locations

Dorman has found that baitfish typically congregate in large schools and stay relatively deep during the cold-water period. "On Santee-Cooper," he explains, "large schools of threadfin shad roam the deep, main-lake flats. However, if a severe cold front blows through, they often move to the edge of the river channel."

The best flats, he says, are those adjacent to a deep river channel that has an old creekbed and/or a ditch running into it. The depth ranges from 25 to 45 feet. Using his graph, he combs the flats looking for large shad schools.

One particularly good location on a flat is a point formed by the intersection of two ditches or creeks. "The depth change between the ditches and flat may be very subtle, say, as little as 3 to 4 feet," he explains. "But that's enough. When baitfish hold over or near that structure, the biggest blues are usually along the edge."

The big blues park themselves underneath the umbrella of baitfish. In most cases, the cats stay near the bottom and swim up to feed. But there are times when they suspend just below the bait.

Often, the schools of shad are so thick they blacken the graph's screen. When Dorman runs across a "black out," he immediately searches for the edge of the school.

"When you find a school of baitfish that large," he says, "locating that outside edge is the secret to finding the biggest catfish relating to it."

Spring Locations

As spring approaches and the water warms, blues begin moving toward their spawning areas. By the time the water temperature reaches the mid 50s, you'll find some of the fish in coves and tributaries, but many of them remain in the main lake, seeking out shallow humps, ridges and points adjacent to deep water.

The ideal spawning structure is 4 to 6 feet deep and has a hard sand or clay bottom with plenty of cover such as stumps or brush.

Summer Locations

After the spawn, blues move back to deeper water in search of shad. Surface temperatures continue to rise, and on most lakes, a thermocline forms. Low oxygen levels prevent both predators and prey from venturing down into the depths for long periods, making the thermocline a prime zone for summer fishing.

"Once you figure out the depth of the thermocline, you can eliminate a lot of potential water," says Randall Hall. "Blues typically suspend just above the thermocline, and they love when it intersects a break or drop-off."

This is Hall's favorite scenario, because it concentrates the action. "When they're in open water, it can be a lot tougher to find them," he explains.

Both Dorman and Hall look for secondary structural features that intersect with the deeper, main-lake channel. They believe the biggest blues hold along ditches or tributary channels (p. 36) during the day and then follow the channels up onto shallower flats after dark.

Sometimes, Hall finds cats suspended over 55- to 60-foot flats with remnant stands of timber. If the thermocline sets up at 35 feet, the fish will suspend in the timber 25 to 30 feet down. "I don't think the catfish are in there for the sake of the wood, though," he says. "They're in there because the shad are, too. In cover or open water, baitfish are the key." If forage is absent, Hall says, even seemingly perfect structure will be devoid of blues.

"You have to look at the entire ecosystem," Hall explains. "The plankton determine where the shad will be and the shad determine where the big blues are."

Fall Locations

In early fall, locational patterns are pretty much the same as in summer. But when the water temperature drops back into the 60s, look for blue cats at the mouths of large coves and creeks. They position themselves on key structural elements like humps, flats and points as they wait for the cooling water to push baitfish (shad, crappies and white bass) out of the coves and creek arms.

It's not unusual to find a number of small "pods" of blues feeding actively in a creek mouth. These pods, which consist mainly of large blues, may be only 10 or 15 yards apart.

"The fish in these pods typically run 30, 40, and 50 pounds," says Randall Hall. "You can be drifting quietly across a point and suddenly you make contact with a pod. We've had four rods all hooked up with fish bigger than 20 pounds."

A sensitive graph is a must for locating shad schools (1) and blues (2) in open water.

Prime Locations for Open-Water Blues

Look for blues in an area of a flat that has a depression, usually from a tributary stream, connecting with the old river channel.

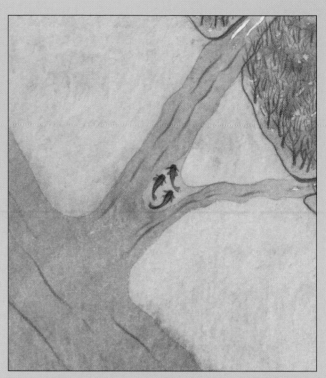

The intersection of a tributary and a smaller ditch, both crossing a flat, is a prime blue cat location.

Blues commonly suspend in stands of flooded timber, almost always at the same depth as schools of shad.

The extended lip of a point at the mouth of a creek channel makes an ideal spot for blues to ambush baitfish moving out of the creek arm in fall.

FISHING FOR OPEN-WATER BLUES

Dorman and Hall employ a variety of methods for open-water blues, depending mainly on the type of structure and cover they're fishing. Here are the techniques they use most often, including their favorite rigs and baits.

Fishing the Flats

When blues are scattered over large flats, drifting is the most effective fishing method because it enables you to cover a lot of water and locate the fish.

You can use a variety of rigs for drifting, ranging from a simple slip-sinker rig (Dorman's favorite) to a "go-to"

Precision drifting with the aid of drift sock and trolling motor is a deadly method for open-water blues.

Equipment for Open-Water Blues

Fishing for blue cats in the open-water expanses of a big reservoir requires some specialized equipment that may not be necessary on smaller waters. Here are some items sure to improve your success:

•**GPS.** With a GPS unit, you can stay on a concentration of fish without having to toss out a marker and advertise your good fortune to other anglers. And you'll be able to return right to the same spot on your next outing.

•**Rod Holders.** Well-designed rod holders allow for quick and easy access to the rod, giving you a solid hookset. When fishing vertically, use rod holders that keep the rods in a horizontal position; when flatlining, holders that keep the rods at a 25- to 45-degree angle are a better choice.

•**Drift Sock(s).** It pays to carry drift socks (sea anchors) in a variety of sizes to control your drift speed in open, windswept waters. In a light wind, a 54-inch drift sock will do the job, but in a stiff gale, you may need one as large as 106 inches. Models with a second rope to pull in the rear of the bag makes retrieving the sock much easier.

•**Trolling Motor.** You'll need a small gas-powered "kicker" or a high-thrust electric motor to control your speed when drifting, and to keep your boat on the desired drift path. Without a trolling motor, it would be impossible to keep your lines close to vertical.

•**Rod and Reel.** A medium- to medium-heavy power, 7-foot baitcasting rod along with an Ambassadeur 5500C reel and 30-pound mono makes a good all-around outfit when you're fishing in open water with few snags. If your rod is too stiff, the fish will feel too much resistance and drop the bait. When you're fishing around woody cover, however, a beefier rod with 50- to 80-pound-test superline is a better choice. Be sure to select a rod with a long handle so it can be set in a rod holder.

Adjustable rod holders have a tension knob that enables you to set the rod at practically any angle.

rig (Hall's favorite, p. 39). Both anglers rely on chunks of cut bait for most of their fishing.

Normally, the rig is fished vertically but, when cats move up on shallow structure to spawn, "flatlining" (letting your lines trail behind the boat) works better because it keeps your bait away from the boat to minimize spooking.

Keeping your lines vertical may not be as easy as it sounds, especially when you're fishing in a stiff wind on a wide-open body of water. To keep your boat drifting slowly along the desired track, you'll need a trolling motor of a suitable size for your boat used in combination with one or two drift socks.

Often, you'll be drifting across a flat when two or three rods spring to life at the same time. When that happens, mark the spot carefully and, once you land the fish, motor back upwind and anchor up.

Work the school until the bite slows and then resume drifting.

Fishing for Suspended Blues

If the fish are suspended just a few feet off the bottom, try the go-to rig described on the next page. Using a leader as long as 10 feet, it's possible to keep your bait as much as 3 feet off the bottom.

But a go-to rig is of little use when the fish are suspended 30 feet off the bottom, as they sometimes are when they're chasing shad in the tops of flooded trees. In this situation, try a sliding balloon rig baited with cut bait (shad, herring, buffalo or carp) or whole shad.

The idea is to set the depth of the balloon to keep the bait just above the level of the fish. With a good depth finder, you'll be able to see the fish and set your depth accordingly. If the fish are concentrated,

toss out your anchor and cover the area thoroughly with the balloon rigs. If they're scattered, spread your balloon lines as far as possible using your rod holders and let the boat drift to cover a wide swath of water.

Fishing for Blues on Structure

When blues are relating to a specific structural element, such as a ditch that intersects the main river channel, the usual open-water drifting tactics are not the answer. If the fish are feeding, you should be able to spot them with your depth finder and hover directly over them, putting your cut bait right in their face.

If the fish are tightly concentrated, motor well upwind of the best spot and toss out an anchor. Set one line on the top of the break, another on the bottom and a third on the slope in between. Place your

How to Control Your Drift

Tie a drift sock to your bow eye; it should keep your boat drifting crosswise to the wind. If you're still drifting too fast, tie on a larger drift sock or tie a second drift sock to a cleat near your transom.

Use your trolling motor or a small outboard to adjust your drift path to keep your boat drifting through the fish zone. If you're fishing breaklines, select those that are aligned with the prevailing wind so you don't have to make major adjustments.

rods in rod holders, set the clickers and wait for a bite. Normally, you won't have to wait too long.

The line positioned closest to the junction with the thermocline is likely to see the most action, but the deepest line generally accounts for the biggest blues.

Anchor your boat above the middle of the break and then toss out one line to fish shallower, one to fish deeper and one to fish directly beneath the boat. Most anglers use cut bait on an ordinary slip-sinker rig.

Special Rigs for Open-Water Blues

The Go-To Rig. *Tie an ordinary slip-sinker rig using an egg sinker and a barrel swivel as a stop, but add a Styrofoam crappie float to the leader. Peg the float in place and then adjust its position to lift the bait to the level of the cats.*

Sliding Balloon Rig. *Tie a slip-float rig as you normally would, but substitute a party balloon for the slip float. Inflate the balloon to softball size, tie it off, clip a large snap-swivel above the knot and then thread your line through the swivel as shown.*

Tips for Fishing with Shad

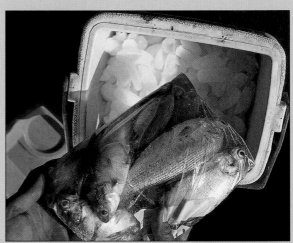

Keep your shad fresh by placing them in a Zip-loc bag and storing them in a cooler on a bed of ice. Without the bag, the shad would soak up too much water and get mushy.

Nose-hook a live 6- to 10-inch gizzard shad on a size 6/0 wide-bend or circle hook when there's a chance of catching stripers mixed in with blues in open water. Stripers won't strike dead or cut bait.

A BULLHEAD PRIMER

by Tom Carpenter

No fish gets less respect than a bullhead, but these lowly members of the catfish clan have a loyal following. And for good reason: You don't need thousands of dollars worth of equipment to chase bullheads, or fancy and complicated rigs. A boat is optional equipment most of the year, a fancy boat totally unnecessary. Best of all, you don't need to travel to exotic locales to find good fishing.

Bullhead fishing is the ultimate in low-stress angling. Once you're at or on the water, the pressure is off; chances are the fish are biting and you're just plain having fun. It's a sport jam packed with simple, nonstop action.

But there is yet another reason why bullheads are worthy of your angling attention: Once you fry up a mess of them you'll understand.

You can find bullheads in practically every kind of warmwater lake or stream, from the tiniest farm ponds to massive bays of the Great Lakes, and from little creeks you could almost jump across to the country's biggest river systems.

Compared to most other members of the catfish family, bullheads can tolerate a much wider range of environmental conditions. You'll find them in the clearest lakes, using the same structure as walleyes and smallmouth bass, but they can also be found in water where the visibility is practically zero.

The bullhead's amazing ability to tolerate low oxygen

It's hard to find a warmwater lake, pond or stream that doesn't have bullheads.

levels explains how it can live in waters unsuitable to most other fish. In shallow, fertile farm-country lakes, for example, the oxygen level often falls so low in winter that bass, panfish and most other gamefish perish. But not bullheads; they can tolerate oxygen levels approaching zero and have even been known to burrow into the mud on a lake bottom, entering a state of near-hibernation until oxygen levels are restored the following spring.

In fact, the bullhead's unbelievable toughness creates problems for fisheries managers. In lakes prone to freeze-out, bullheads gain the upper hand, and the only way these waters can be managed for other fish is by removing the bullheads with chemicals and then restocking.

Bottom line: No matter where you live in the United States or southern Canada, chances are you can find fishable numbers of one of the "big three" bullhead species (black, brown or yellow) within a short distance of your home. If you don't have a clue about where to start looking, just ask around. It's not like trying to get someone to reveal their favorite bass or walleye spot.

But even as simple as bullhead fishing is, there are some things you need to know to guarantee success. On the pages that follow, we'll explain where to find bullheads throughout the year, show you some time-proven methods and baits, and detail some important differences between the three major species.

A BULLHEAD YEAR

Even though bullheads are easy to find and catch, especially in spring, you still have to know where to find concentrations of fish.

And what about summer and fall? Bullheads don't receive as much attention then because they're much more difficult to locate; catching a mess of fish isn't such a cakewalk.

So let's take a look at the bullhead's year and identify some of the best locations to fish in each season.

Spring

In early spring, when a few sunny days start raising the water's surface temperature, bullheads move from their deeper winter haunts into shallow areas of a lake or river. This kicks off the best bullhead fishing of the year, and the action gets even better as the water continues to warm into spring.

Good bullhead locations now include boat channels, canals, backwater lakes, sloughs, sluggish feeder creeks—most any protected, still water that is connected to (and warms faster than) the main lake or river.

If these "connecting" types of habitat don't exist on your favorite bullhead lake, look at a lake map: Find the shallowest bay, preferably one exposed to the full daytime sun, and fish there. In rivers and creeks, look for lowhead dams and other structures that block upstream fish movement.

Although you'll often find springtime bullheads in mucky, soft-bottomed bays and backwaters, don't get the idea that they're always associated with soft bottoms. On the contrary, they much prefer a firmer bottom when available. One of my all-time favorite spring bullhead spots is a sandy swimming beach. The shallow water warms quickly in spring, drawing baitfish and invertebrates … with foraging bullheads close behind. As an added bonus, the firm, clean bottom is good for keeping your rig free of debris and snags.

Summer

How often have you been fishing deeper water for summertime panfish, walleyes or even bass, got a good bite and hauled in a big old bullhead?

Prime Bullhead Locations

Boat canals and other channels connected to the main lake warm up quickly in spring, drawing minnows and activating invertebrates which, in turn, attract bullheads.

Shallow bays are the main springtime bullhead hangouts on most lakes. To find active bullheads, look for a bay with a warm breeze blowing right into it (arrow).

It happens all the time, proving that bullheads can be just as structure-oriented as the more popular kinds of gamefish—and just as challenging to find during the summer months. Now a boat, basic depthfinder and lake or river map come in handy for helping you locate bullheads.

In lakes, summer bullheads usually relate to weed edges and depth changes. One of my favorite summertime bullhead spots is a shallow, weed-topped hump that rises out of deeper water.

But don't get the idea that you can't find summertime bullheads if you're shore-bound. Just look for weedlines and other weed edges close to the shoreline, especially around points that give the fish easy access to both deep and shallow water. Notice the common factor in all these spots: shallow-water feeding areas near deeper daytime holding areas.

In rivers, head for deep, slackwater holes. Bends are good too, but don't expect to find bullheads in the swift current on the outside of the bend. Unlike some of the larger catfish species, they won't tolerate much current, so they're much more likely to be in the slower water along the edge of a sandbar on the opposite side of the river or in the eddy that forms downstream of the bar.

In either case, bullheads usually stay in the deeper water during the day and then move up on an adjacent flat to feed around sunset and into the night.

Fall

If you get the urge to chase bullheads in autumn, look in the same places you would in springtime—warm, shallow bays and flats. Bullheads seldom frequent the "connecting" waters now like they did in spring, but will instead stay in waters that allow a quick retreat to the main lake or river once the cold weather hits.

Winter

You may catch an occasional bullhead in lakes that don't freeze up in winter, but it's a real rarity to pull a bullhead through an ice hole.

If you're an avid bullheader, winter is a good time to dream of those first warm spring nights when, once again, lanterns hiss and open water laps gently against the shore.

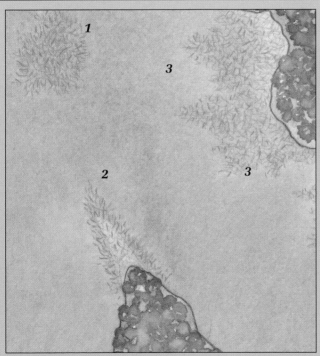

Main-lake structure such as (1) a shallow weedy hump, (2) a weedy point with an extended underwater lip and (3) an irregular weedline are key summertime bullhead locations.

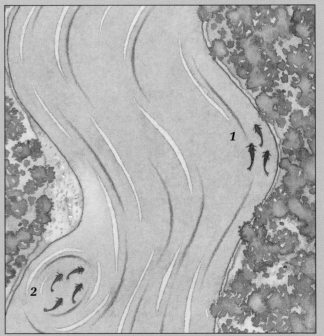

Deep outside bends (1) in a river or stream hold bullheads most of the year, assuming the current is relatively light. The eddy (2) that forms below the bar on the opposite side of the river is also a good place to look.

HOW TO CATCH BULLHEADS

Even if you take the time to check all your old fishing magazines and all your fishing books, you'll be hard-pressed to find any kind of story on bullheads, let alone one that gives you any solid information on how to catch them.

Luckily, these cooperative feeders aren't too demanding; you can make plenty of mistakes and still bring home a nice mess of whiskerfish. Here's a quick rundown on the basic gear, baits and methods.

Tackle & Rigs

Most any medium-power spinning, spincasting or baitcasting outfit will do the job. Opt for 10-pound line—it won't reduce the number of bites you get from aggressive bullheads, and it will help you pull out of snags.

Long-shank hooks (size 2 to 1/0) are a must for bullhead fishing. Often as not, a bullhead swallows the bait, and a long-shank hook gives you something to grab. Even so, you'll need a needlenose pliers or disgorger to remove the most deeply embedded hooks.

Most bullheading is done using bottom-fishing rigs. Just tie on a hook and then add a ¼- to 1-ounce Rubber-Cor or dog-ear sinker 12 to 18 inches up the line. In shallow water, you can get by with a couple of big split shot. If you really want to go "high-tech," make a slip-sinker rig using an egg or bullet sinker. Such finesse is usually not necessary, however; a bullhead is not likely to drop the bait just because it feels a little resistance.

If there is a layer of moss or weeds on the bottom, you'll have to add a float. Use a clip-on or peg-on float in

shallow water (5 feet or less) or a slip-float in deeper water. Add just enough weight to balance the float, and set it so the bait just skims the top of the vegetation.

Baits

Hungry bullheads pass up few meals—alive or dead—so you shouldn't have any trouble finding baits that work.

Garden worms and nightcrawlers are the old standbys. Gob one crawler or a couple of garden worms onto your hook, leaving the ends dangling. Standard channel catfish baits work well too—stinkbaits of all kinds, doughbaits, smelly cheese concoctions and bloodbaits. Cut bait will also catch fish, as will dead or live minnows. When using small crappie minnows, try two or even three on a hook.

Why Bullheading? *by Tom Carpenter*

When I was a boy, I'd come home from school on a warm early-spring day thinking that fishing season would never start. As if he knew, my dad would say "Get out the poles." So after dinner we'd go bullheading on one of several red-sand coves on Zander's Lake. What an adventure—fishing in the gathering darkness and early night.

I remember sitting there in the lantern light, waiting for my rod tip to start bobbing again, a 5-gallon bucket half full of yellow-bellied bullheads sloshing about and just waiting for an addition. One night we watched 3 deer come down to the water's edge to drink at sunset, and another night we got caught in a great storm, running a mile back to our car with lightning flashes showing us the way. I double-handed the big bucket all the way, and all 27 well-agitated bullheads made it to our cleaning table.

By college, when trout, big crappies, taverns and girls beckoned me in springtime, I still found time to go home and chase bullheads. Even then something so simple meant something good and needed.

And now, with many years behind me and sons of my own, bullheads represent something fun and different—another opportunity, with fishing action and little nighttime adventures, to further hook my boys on the outdoors. In the lantern light, I can see myself in their eyes.

And I suspect that at the tail end of my fishing career, bullhead fishing will mean something too: visits to people and times of my past that I don't want to forget.

Bullheading is great family fun—pass it on!

In summer, have some fun catching grasshoppers and crickets with the kids; the bugs make excellent bullhead baits as do grub worms and other kinds of immature insects. Another top-rate bullhead bait is a wiggly leech.

Fishing Methods

Bullhead fishing is the height of simplicity. Toss out one of the bottom rigs described, place your rod in a forked stick or rod holder and wait for a bite, usually a rat-tat-tat or tug at your rod tip. Give the fish a couple of seconds, then set the hook. If you wait too long, the hook will be so far down the fish's gullet that you won't be able to see it. When float fishing, keep your bait just brushing the bottom or weedtops—bullheads aren't likely to swim up very far to get a meal.

Because bullheads are so aggressive, it's usually a mistake to "wait them out." If you don't get a bite within a few minutes, reel in and cast out to a different spot. Keep moving until you locate the fish.

"Trophy Bullheads"

In most waters with high bullhead populations, the fish range from $1/2$ to 1 pound. But if you're after something bigger (2 pounds or more), look to waters with much lower bullhead numbers. This usually means heading for lakes or rivers with good populations of predators like walleyes, pike, bass or big cats to keep bullhead numbers in check. In fact, you'll often find the best bullhead fishing in the same spots that hold these predator fish.

SKINNY-WATER CATS

by Kurt Beckstrom

Finding channel cats in a river is easy: Just look for a deep, slow-moving stretch of water with a sand, gravel or rubble bottom. At least that's the standard wisdom shared by most veteran catmen.

But that's not what you'll hear from Stu McKay, owner of Cats on the Red, a guide service catering to anglers who want to enjoy the world-class catfish action to be found in the Red River of the North.

"Probably the biggest misconception about catfish is that you only find them in the deep part of a river," says McKay. "That's where most anglers get thrown off, because it's just not true a lot of the time."

It's not that the deep slots and holes are not a good choice; in many cases, they are. But they're not the only place on the river to catch channel cats. McKay commonly finds the fish in water so shallow he can touch bottom with his rod tip.

Not only are these shallow-water hot spots ignored by most anglers, they offer some of the easiest catfishing to be found anywhere. That's because the fish are in the shallows for only one reason: to feed.

And shallow-water cats make an ideal target for shore fishermen. In fact, the cats are often so close to shore that you can fish them from the bank more easily than you can from a boat!

The Red River of the North:
North America's Best Channel Cat River?

The Red River of the North forms the boundary between North Dakota and Minnesota before flowing northward into Manitoba. The river, particularly the Manitoba portion, supports one of the continent's premier channel cat fisheries. Fish exceeding 30 pounds are brought to net every year, and it's not unusual to spend an entire day catching and releasing 15- to 25-pounders.

The main reason the Red River produces such hefty cats is that the fish spend the colder months roaming the wide expanses of Lake Winnepeg, which is the 13th-largest lake in the world. The big lake has minimal sportfishing pressure and an abundance of forage, an ideal combination for growing catfish of gigantic proportions.

In spring, catfish move out of the lake and begin swimming upriver to spawn. Their upstream migration is blocked by the St. Andrews Lock & Dam at Lockport, about 30

miles above the lake. The fish remain in the river all summer and well into the fall, scattering throughout the river once spawning has been completed.

The character of the river between the St. Andrews Lock & Dam and the lake (Stu McKay's favorite reach) differs greatly from the Minnesota-North Dakota portion of the river. The riverbed consists of rock, gravel and sand rather than the muck and mud that dominate the upper reaches. Because of the hard bottom, the river produces an abundance of channel cat forage, including mooneyes and goldeyes. These baitfish have a high fat content and any fish that eat them grow rapidly.

Manitoba regulations require anglers to release any cat longer than 24 inches and to use barbless hooks. These restrictions should ensure that the Red River's trophy-cat reputation remains intact for years to come.

SEASONAL LOCATIONS

In the Red River, like many other rivers that feed large lakes, most of the cats spend the winter months in the lake—in this case, Lake Winnipeg. But soon after ice-out, the fish begin their upstream migration. Their movement is blocked by the first dam—in this case, the St. Andrews Dam at Lockport.

There, action in the tailrace area can be spectacular. But once the fish actually start to spawn, they usually move back downriver, leaving many anglers scratching their heads.

Because the Red River is at the extreme northern edge of the channel cat's range, the fish spawn in much cooler water than they do farther south.

"I've seen channels spawning when the water is in the mid-50s," McKay notes, "but usually it occurs from the high 50s to mid-60s."

Once the fish leave the tailrace area to spawn, they seek out shoreline flats maybe 50 to 75 feet wide that run from a depth of about 8 feet right

The St. Andrews Dam at Lockport is the focus of the early-season catfish action.

The Importance of Riprap

Why is riprap so attractive to catfish? Research by hydraulic engineers provides the answer.

Current measurements through the entire water column of a river show that even a smooth bottom has a zone of slower water above it. Engineers attribute this to the "friction" between the water and the riverbed. It's not unusual to find a current speed of 3 or 4 feet per second in midwater and only 1 foot per second near the bottom.

The slow-water zone increases in thickness as the roughness of the substrate (river's bottom) increases.

The slow-water area associated with riprap is easily thick enough to provide an adequate comfort zone for large catfish.

The slower current is also ideal for a variety of aquatic life including invertebrates and forage fish. Fisheries researchers on the Mississippi River, for example, commonly find large numbers of gizzard shad along main channel riprap banks. Normally associated with slack-water habitats, the shad find shelter from the current by hovering just above the riprap.

Nooks and crannies in the rocks also support high densities of aquatic invertebrates such as crayfish, freshwater shrimp, insect larvae and freshwater mussels. These invertebrates provide food not only for catfish, but for other forage fish upon which the catfish feed.

Riprap consisting of large, irregular chunks of broken rock makes better fish habitat than riprap made up of small or smooth rocks. Not only do the larger chunks create a thicker zone of slow water, they won't wash away in a severe flood.

up to the shoreline. Some areas are only 50 or 60 feet long, others extend for more than 1,000 feet. Many of the best flats have a riprap bank and bottom. Riprap slows the current and concentrates forage species.

You'll often find incredible numbers of catfish concentrated on these flats, not only at spawning time but through the summer and well into the fall. You may even find some cats on the flats during the pre-spawn period. On a good day, you can easily catch 75 to 100.

"They're either there, or they're not," says McKay, "and when you find them, they're active. These are overlooked and underfished waters."

McKay discovered this hidden treasure years ago while guiding some clients for white bass. "The wind was blowing hard into the bank and we were using ultra-light gear, throwing small Rapalas up to the shoreline," he recalls. "We'd caught a couple of whites when my fisherman hooked a cat that spooled him. While that was going, I hooked one, too."

In the ensuing chaos, McKay didn't notice that his boat was drifting dangerously close to the bank. Until, that is, the electric motor housing started banging on the rocks. Then, it seemed like the world exploded.

"The noise caused a massive eruption of giant channel cats heading for deep water," he says. "They were boiling out of the shallows for 100 yards, maybe 150. There's no way to explain it. You would have to have seen it to believe it. That was the first inkling that these channel cats used such shallow water."

Prime Red River Catfish Locations

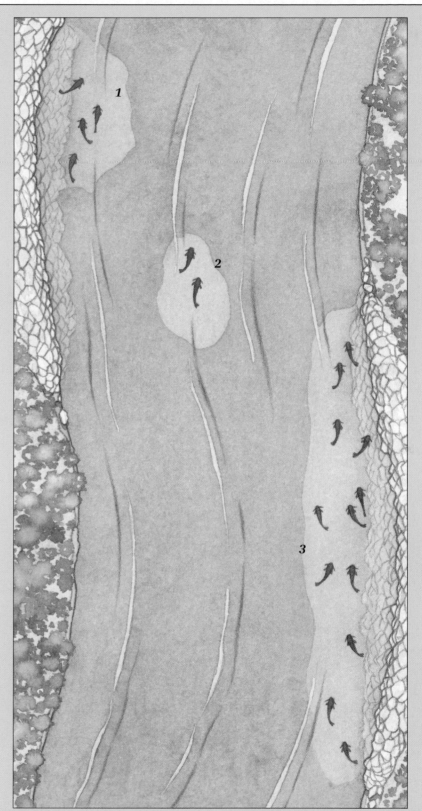

Look for catfish on **(1)** small shoreline flats, **(2)** rocky midriver humps and **(3)** long shoreline flats. The best flats have riprap banks and a rocky bottom.

How to Catch Skinny-Water Cats

"The key is to keep moving until you find fish," McKay explains. "You may not have to move far, just enough to cover new water."

Since channel cats could be prowling anywhere on the flat, from the lip of the main-channel ledge right up to the shoreline, covering water is critical. And though they may form pods, where you'll catch a number of fish from a single spot, those pods may be scattered too.

If you don't get on fish right away, McKay recommends moving to another spot. "The worst thing you can do is overstay your welcome," he says. "I get edgy after 5 minutes, and about the longest I stick with one spot is 15 minutes, 20 at the outside."

"One of the best methods for eliminating nonproductive water is to fish float rigs," says McKay. "With them, you can fish a long stretch of the flat, maybe 200 feet. Just anchor the boat at the head of the flat, and drift the rigs downstream."

From a boat anchored midway between the shoreline and drop-off, McKay can usually cover all depths, working the deeper side more than the shallow. Sometimes, he says, he'll toss bottom rigs when fishing the flats, but not when he wants to probe a large section.

"When bottom-fishing, you make the fish come to you; with floats, you go to the fish."

While McKay wants his bait (generally the head or a 1-inch steak from a goldeye) to drift, he wants it to drift as close to the bottom as possible. It should occasionally bounce off the rocks or gravel as it moves with the current, without hanging up. "When you get the system down, you can make it hug the bottom, but you won't lose a lot of terminal gear," he says.

From his anchored boat, he either sends the rig straight downstream or makes a gentle lob-cast to the side and feeds line as the float moves away. While it may require a little manipulation with the rod tip, the rig usually holds its course, which means the bait has covered a particular depth for the entire drift.

To maintain control of the float rig, and to ensure solid hooksets at long distances, McKay uses a rod that's at least 8 feet long. His current favorite is the Berkley ReFlex in medium-heavy action (RFC802), matched with an Ambassadeur 6500 filled with 25- to 30-pound Big Game monofilament.

"Rod action isn't as important as length," he says. "You have to be able to pick up a lot of line on the set, and a shorter rod won't do it."

"When these fish take a bait, the float just disappears; I mean it's gone! Don't wait; don't feed line, just set the hook. And when you do, you're in for a fight. Because the water is so shallow, the fish has nowhere to go but away from you, and it's usually toward deeper water."

With the likelihood that a catfish may be a half block away when you sink the barb, it's logical that a low-stretch superline would come in handy. For some anglers, maybe, but McKay prefers to stick with mono. Its stretch factor is more beneficial during a shallow-water fight, he explains, than a low-stretch line is on the hookset.

Stu McKay and a hefty, skinny-water channel cat from the Red River.

"It's extremely rare that you don't hook 'em up," he says.

Fishing the entire width of the flat entails nothing more than sliding the float up or down the line and making longer or shorter casts to the side. Each drift covers another depth range. And it's sometimes impossible to go too shallow, according to McKay.

"Sometimes we cast so close to shore, the bait often lands on a rock and we have to pull it off into the current."

In most river fishing situations, current breaks play a major role in fish location, especially when the holding zone is close to shore. But McKay says it's not a real factor on the flats he fishes. "You don't get much of a current seam, so you don't have to be as picky about where to position the bait. The fish could be anywhere, so you may have to search the entire flat."

How to Make & Fish a Float Rig

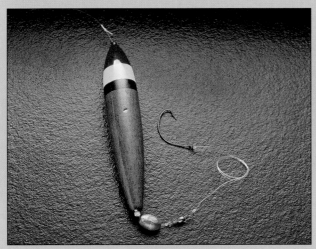

1 Attach a bobber stop to your line, then thread on a bead, a large cigar float and a ³/₈- to ³/₄-ounce egg sinker. Tie on a barrel swivel to reduce line twist and act as a sinker stop. Complete the rig by tying on an 8- to 10-inch leader (snipped from the main line) and attaching a size 2/0 to 3/0 wide-bend hook.

2 Push the hook point through the "meat side" of a goldeye steak just above the spine and bring it out the skin side about a third of the way down from the top of the back, as shown. This ensures that the point remains exposed, and the bait doesn't fill up the hook gap.

3 Cover a wide swath of water on a flat by drifting several float rigs. The angler on the inside casts toward shore and then points his rod shoreward to keep the float rig drifting close to shore. The angler on the outside casts toward midstream and points his rod in that direction to cover deeper water. The angler in the middle floats his rig directly behind the boat.

TAILWATER HEAVYWEIGHTS

by Keith Sutton

If you ask a seasoned cat-man where he would go if he absolutely had to catch a trophy-class catfish, chances are his answer would be "The tailwaters of a big-river dam."

It's easy to understand why big cats of all kinds love tailwaters: At every dam on every river, there's a piscatorial smorgasbord awaiting them.

The exact items on the menu vary from river to river, but that doesn't really matter. A trophy-class catfish will take just about any kind of fish that will fit into its mouth.

In southern catfish rivers, the prime fare is likely to be shad and skipjack herring. In some cases, these baitfish are washed down from above the dam and wind up crippled or

dead after passing through the turbines. Cats gather like kids 'round an ice-cream truck, gobbling every morsel that swims or drifts near.

Farther north, cats may dine on suckers, chubs, sheepshead, goldeyes, carp, bluegills and dozens of other finny delicacies that are drawn to the swirling current.

Increasing springtime flows draw baitfish to the tailwaters and the catfish are not far behind. Later in spring, they may drop back downriver to spawn in backwater areas off the main channel, but once spawning has been completed, many of the fish return to the tailwaters to begin a feeding binge that lasts well into fall and possibly winter.

The term "tailwaters" generally refers to the fast-water zone immediately below a dam, but that's not the only reach that holds catfish. As a rule, you'll want to focus on the first mile or two of water below the dam.

To simplify the process of finding and catching cats, it helps to divide the tailwater area into three sections: the whitewater reach, the middle reach and the lower reach (below). The length and breadth of each section varies considerably depending on the type of dam and the river's size, but you should be able to identify each of these water types on the rivers you fish.

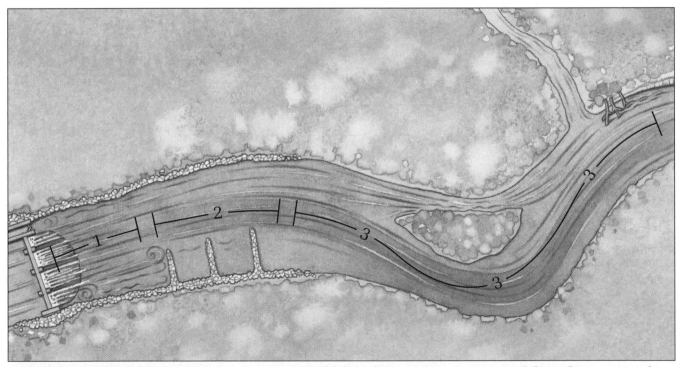

Tailwater zones include (1) the whitewater zone, which is the uppermost portion of the tailwater near the dam and adjacent structures; (2) the middle reach, which begins where churning water from the dam starts smoothing out and slowing down; and (3) the lower reach, which begins where man-made structures are replaced by natural habitat.

Fishing in the whitewater zone peaks during periods of high flow.

LOCATING TAILWATER CATS

Depending on the river, you may find up to three species of catfish in the tailwaters zone. Of course, they won't all share the same spots because of differences in their current tolerance. As in any river, blue cats prefer the fastest current and flatheads, the slowest, with channels favoring current of intermediate speed. Here are some tips for finding catfish in each of the three tailwater reaches.

The Whitewater Zone

At first glance, the swirling, frothy water immediately below a dam appears to be too fast to hold catfish. But experienced catmen know better; in fact, the whitewater zone consistently produces some of the most impressive trophies.

The larger catfish generally lay claim to the prime feeding locations. As a rule, they look for spots where they can rest in slower water alongside a faster moving run—the same spots that draw scads of baitfish.

One of the very best locations is a "groove" or "current tunnel"—a zone of slower-moving water between gates of the dam. These spots are easy to recognize and usually see little fishing pressure.

Most dams have several gates, and you have to try more than one of them to find the fish. Remember that water flow through a dam may change several times a day as power requirements or water levels demand, causing the fish to shift position to find a comfort zone, and you may have to adjust your boat position to stay with them.

Another important spot is a washout hole, which is a depression scoured in the river bottom by the force of water tumbling over the dam apron (p. 58). Some of these holes, however, are off limits to boaters, so make sure you know the regulations. Even if you can't anchor there, you may be able to anchor downstream and cast into the hole.

If there are large eddies immediately below the dam alongside the fast current, they'll almost certainly hold catfish. Often the water in these eddies is actually flowing back toward the dam, creating a swirling pool that teems with baitfish.

Remember that constant water flow through the dam is necessary to maintain good catfishing conditions in the whitewater reach. Should conditions force dam operators to close all gates, catfishing success will take a nosedive. The best fishing generally coincides with periods of highest water flow, when most or all gates are open.

The Middle Reach

Fishing in the middle reach peaks during periods of reduced water flow through the dam. If one or more gates are closed, cats feeding in the whitewater zone often move to structure in the middle reaches. They continue feeding there until water flow is restored to higher levels.

The key to finding catfish in the middle reaches is to locate structure that breaks

When current flow through the dam subsides, cats slip downstream into the middle reach.

Prime fishing areas in the lower reach are pretty much the same as those on any free-flowing stretch of a big river: deep holes on outside bends, especially those with timber or other woody cover; deep chutes; bridge channels; rock, gravel and sandbars; logjams; and side channels connecting the main river with backwaters and oxbow lakes.

Pay special attention to any good-sized tributaries. Catfish sometimes swim up tributaries to spawn, and they often congregate around tributary mouths during pre-spawn and post-spawn periods. In summer, cats may congregate around the inflow from a tributary when flow in the main channel is minimal.

If there's a deep hole where the tributary meets the main channel, it could be an important wintering area, particularly if the hole has plenty of woody cover to break the current.

the current and attracts schools of baitfish.

In many cases, the fish congregate around wing dams (also called wing dikes), which are long, narrow man-made rock structures that usually protrude from the water and direct the current toward the middle of the river. Wing dams were constructed to prevent the main channel from silting in and reduce shoreline erosion, but they offer a made-to-order feeding station for many gamefish, including catfish.

You'll generally catch the most catfish along the current seam formed by the water deflecting off the wing dam's upper lip, but there will be times when you'll find cats in the deep scour hole below the wing dam as well.

Humps, rock piles and boulders in the middle reach also draw cats. Watch your depth finder closely to find any sudden rise, and look for changes in the current pattern that may reveal the location of shallow structure. Often you'll see a boil on the surface just downstream of the obstruction. Cats relate to these structures in much the same way they relate to a wing dam, feeding primarily along the upstream lip.

The Lower Reach

When conditions in the upper sections of the tailwaters are ideal, the downstream reach may be almost devoid of large cats. But when the flow is extremely low, usually in summer and fall, catfish may hang out in the lower reach for weeks on end.

The lower section of the tailwaters, which looks pretty much like any free-flowing river, is a good choice during low-water periods.

Prime Catfish Spots in the Tailwater Zone

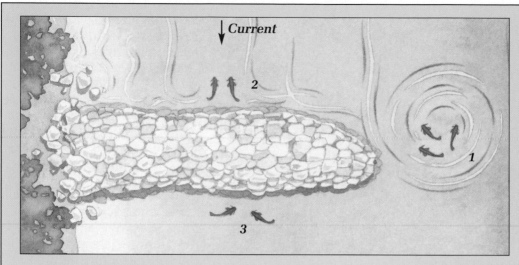

Wing Dam. *Current flowing down the main river channel strikes the wing dam and is deflected toward midriver, forming a **(1)** large eddy at the end of the wing dam that usually holds catfish. Some cats also hold along **(2)** the front lip of the wing dam and in **(3)** the scour hole just downstream.*

Grooves. *These slack-water zones form below the concrete structures that separate the gates of a big-river dam. Catfish position themselves along the entire length of a groove.*

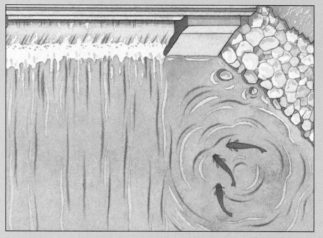

Eddies Below Dam. *Large eddies often form alongside the swift current immediately below a big-river dam. These eddies often teem with baitfish—and big cats.*

Washout Hole. *The powerful force of water cascading over the apron of the dam scours out a hole immediately below the dam. This hole may be more than 50 feet deep. Washout holes often hold large blues.*

Tributary Mouth. *Catfish often swim up good-sized tributaries to spawn but, prior to and after spawning, you'll find them around tributary mouths. If there is a deep washout hole below the tributary, cats may winter there.*

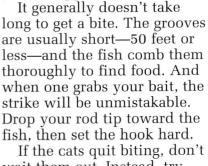

You'll soon develop the "feel" necessary to know exactly what's happening.

It generally doesn't take long to get a bite. The grooves are usually short—50 feet or less—and the fish comb them thoroughly to find food. And when one grabs your bait, the strike will be unmistakable. Drop your rod tip toward the fish, then set the hook hard.

If the cats quit biting, don't wait them out. Instead, try another groove.

Using a sidearm lob cast, toss your 3-way rig (below) into the upstream end of a groove. Feed line as the rig sinks to the bottom and then take up the slack as the rig drifts slowly back to you. When you feel a take or anything out of the ordinary, set the hook.

FISHING THE TAILWATERS

Tailwater anglers must be versatile; because of the wide variety of habitat types in a typical tailwater area, you'll have to employ several different techniques to fish them properly. Here are some suggestions for fishing some of the more common types of tailwater habitat.

Grooves

To fish a groove, anchor just downstream of it, where the current speed starts to pick up. Toss a 3-way rig (right) and some cut bait toward the dam to reach the head of the groove and then let the rig sink. If you've hit the groove properly, your bait should stop as soon as it hits bottom. If you miss the groove, you'll

feel the bait tumbling back toward you at a fast clip.

The idea is to use a sinker that is just heavy enough to allow the current to drag your bait slowly across the bottom as it drifts down the groove.

Washout Hole or Large Eddy

A jig tipped with cut bait is a good choice in this situation. To fish a washout hole, motor upstream as far as safety permits, then drop the bait to the bottom and crank it up a bit. As your boat drifts, use your motor to maintain a speed that keeps your line as close to vertical as possible. Most strikes will come as you're walking the jig down the upstream lip or up the downstream lip of the hole. Continue drifting until you're on the shelf below the hole,

Make a 3-way rig using a wide-bend hook and a bell sinker. Slice a shad, herring or sucker into 1-inch chunks. Push the hook through the bait as shown, leaving the point exposed (left). If you're having trouble with your rig drifting out of a groove too quickly, substitute a pyramid sinker (right) for the bell sinker. With its flat sides, a pyramid sinker is not as likely to roll with the current.

Fishing a Hole or Eddy

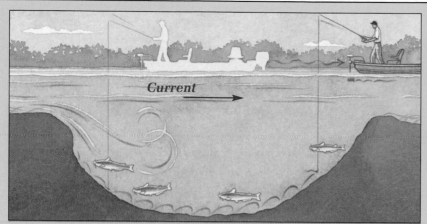

Motor to the upstream lip of the hole, lower your jig to the bottom, then lift it an inch or two to reduce hang-ups. Control your drift speed with your trolling motor, keeping your line as close to vertical as possible until you've drifted over the downstream lip. Motor back upstream and make several more parallel drifts to cover the entire hole.

To effectively fish a hole or eddy, use a jig tipped with cut bait. If that's not working, try baiting up with a whole baitfish before moving on.

then motor back upstream and try another drift.

Your strategy for fishing an eddy is basically the same, but you may have to start at the downstream end in order to drift with the current.

Jigs also work well for fishing humps, rock piles and other structure because you can easily adjust your depth as you move shallower or deeper.

Fishing a Wing Dam

Wing Dam

To fish the current seam along the upstream lip of a wing dam, anchor up and toss out a slip-bobber rig baited with a piece of shad, sucker or herring. Let the moving water carry your float along the seam, presenting the bait to cats lying in wait in the slower water to intercept any food carried to them by the faster water. Surprisingly, the eddy that forms at the end of

a wing dam is not a particularly good fishing spot. Although it may hold some cats, they're generally in a resting rather than feeding mode.

To fish the scour hole below a wing dam, anchor up and toss out a slip-sinker rig with a chunk of cut bait. But be prepared to wait a while for a bite; catfish below the wing dam are seldom as active as those above it.

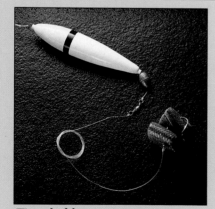

Tie a bobber stop onto your line, thread on a bead and a cigar float, add a Rubber-Cor sinker and a size 1/0 to 4/0 hook, and bait up with a piece of shad, sucker or herring.

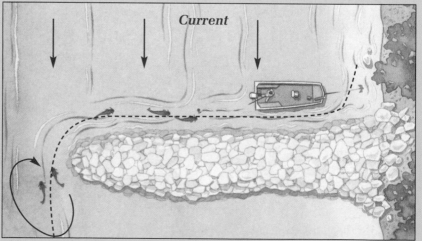

Anchor your boat along the current seam that parallels the upper lip of a wing dam. Toss out a slip-float rig (left) and feed line as it drifts along the current seam (dotted line).

Shore Fishing in the Tailwaters

by Monte Burch

Shore casting is extremely popular in many tailwater areas because you can easily reach some of the best fishing spots even if you don't have a boat.

But to fish from shore effectively, you'll need some specialized equipment. To cast a heavy weight a long distance out into the surging water, then pull and fight a cat that could weigh in excess of 50 pounds out of the rocks and heavy current, you'll need a long, powerful rod. My personal favorite is a 10½-foot, medium-heavy-power Penn Slammer with a Penn 320GTi level-wind reel spooled with 50-pound hard-finish mono.

I can cast this rig over half a football field length and, by changing to 200/60 Spiderwire, I can gain quite a bit more distance. The problem is, the rig tends to tangle on the cast due to the extreme limpness of the line, and when you're hung up—you're really hung up.

The idea is to throw the bait as far as possible out into the channel, propping the rod up on the riprap or setting it into a rod holder

A long, powerful rod is a must when shore fishing in the tailwater zone.

pushed into the ground (below left). Then tighten up your line and wait for a bite.

Hang-ups are a common problem in shore fishing, so most anglers use a 3-way rig with the sinker attached to a fairly light dropper. This way, should the sinker hang up in the rocks, you can break it off without losing the rest of the rig.

Your choice of bait depends on what is the most prevalent in the

area. Where shad are present, they are usually the top pick, but many anglers prefer goldfish, perch, bluegills or cut herring. Be sure to check your local regulations regarding the use of "gamefish" species as bait. As a rule, softer baits such as doughballs and prepared baits are not quite as effective in tailrace waters because the swift current works them off the hook.

Shore-Fishing Tips

Set your rod in a rod holder that has a stake on the bottom to secure it in the ground. If you don't have a rod holder, just prop the rod up on a rock or forked stick and set another rock on the handle so a fish can't pull it into the water.

Use a reel with a bait clicker. This way you can leave the reel disengaged so the fish can take the bait without feeling undue resistance, yet the clicker will signal a bite when the fish starts moving away.

DEEP THINKING FOR RIVER CATS

by Chris Altman

Deep water and catfish go together like soup beans and cornbread. Just ask Tillman "Tim" Collett, a catfish wizard from Lenoir City, Tennessee, who plies his craft virtually every day on the Tennessee River between Fort Loudoun Dam and Watts Bar Lake.

"Deep river holes are the best areas that I have found for producing both numbers of catfish and very large catfish on a consistent, year-round basis," Collett says.

It's tough to locate catfish in a huge impoundment, but finding them in deep river holes is much easier. With nothing more than a simple flasher, an angler can locate these deep-water holes and possibly spot the fish. But even if you can't mark them, you can be pretty confident that the deepest hole in a given stretch of river will hold plenty of cats, especially blues.

Although many anglers are intimidated by the thought of fishing in moving water, the current is really your ally. It causes the fish to position themselves in specific areas, so you can target them more easily.

Deep river holes produce cats throughout the year, but Collett believes they are most productive during the hottest months of summer. The holes are also the best producers during the hottest hours of daylight. "The really big cats will remain in the holes throughout the night," he says, "but I think that the smaller fish leave the holes after dark and move into the shallows where food is more prevalent."

Bob Holmes from Trenton, Tennessee, also guides for cats on the Tennessee River, but his approach for finding cats is a bit different than Tillman's. He looks for "dog-legs"—sharp bends in the river channel where the current flowing into the bank washes out a deep hole.

"The catfish gang up in these areas for a number of reasons," he says, "but primarily because the current washes food to them."

Tim Collett and some nice deepwater cats.

A Tennessee River "dog-leg" cat.

LOCATING DEEP-WATER CATS

It's fairly easy to find cats when they're holed up in their deep hideouts, but there are some tricks that will put you on the fish a little quicker.

Deep Holes

Although Collett knows his favorite stretch of the Tennessee River like a groundhog knows his burrow, he keeps his eyes glued to his depthfinder when running the channel.

"Any deep hole will hold a bunch of catfish," he says, "but the most productive ones generally are rather deep (in relation to the average depth of the river) and full of rocky cover. Catfish love rocks, especially those big craggy rocks that grab your hooks and sinkers."

Collett says that his most productive river holes are generally 30 to 70 feet deep. Keep in mind, however, that in a smaller river, good holes may be much shallower.

Dog-Legs

Bob Holmes finds catfish in practically any dog-leg, but he prefers those that have a clay bank because they tend to have an irregular bottom that provides plenty of catfish hiding spots.

Catfish begin moving into the dog-legs in late June, soon after spawning has been completed, and they'll stay there until September, when they begin to move upstream to tailwater areas.

The first fish to move into the dog-legs can usually be found at a depth of 12 to 18 feet. But as the summer progresses, they rapidly move deeper. By late summer, most catfish are holding at a depth of 35 to 40 feet. "You can catch these cats a little shallower, and you can find them much deeper, but for every fish that I catch above 15 or below 35 feet, I think I can catch 5 or 6 in the water between those depths," Holmes says emphatically.

FISHING TECHNIQUES

How you fish deep-water catfish hideouts depends mainly on the water depth and current pattern. Although Collett and Holmes both

Where to Find Cats in Deep Holes & Dog-Legs

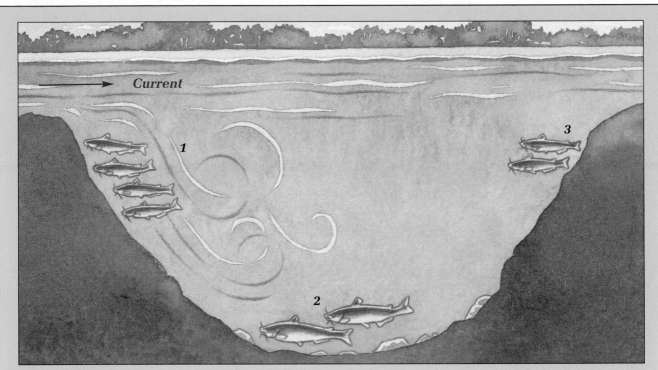

Deep Holes. *The greatest number of catfish, and the most active feeders, are normally found on **(1)** the upstream slope of a deep hole. The biggest cats, however, usually lie in **(2)** the deepest part of the hole. The **(3)** downstream slope also holds a few active feeders.*

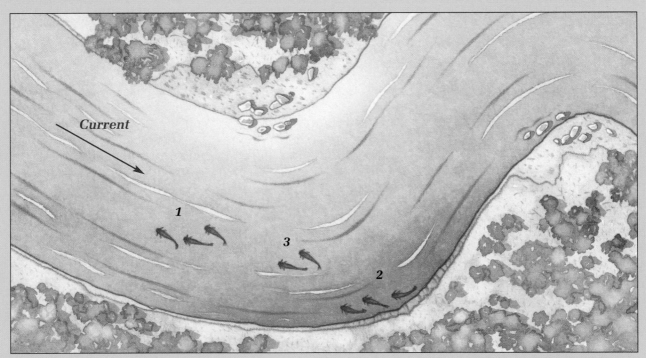

Dog-Legs. *As in a deep hole (top), the largest number of cats hold at the upstream end of a dog-Ieg, especially where the break is sharpest. In late June, when catfish first start congregating in the dog-legs, you'll find most of them at **(1)** depths of 12 to 18 feet. By late summer, most of the fish go much deeper, usually holding at **(2)** depths of 35 feet or more. The best summertime bite, however, is at **(3)** intermediate depths because the catfish there are more active.*

Take the time to map out a deep hole or dog-leg, and you will catch more catfish.

prefer drift-fishing, they go about their business in slightly different ways.

Collett's Method

After "mapping" the hole with his depthfinder to determine its length and width, Collett starts fishing at the upstream end and on one side of the hole. He prefers a drifting, bottom-bouncing technique.

"The idea is to keep the bait directly underneath the boat as you drift slowly downstream," Collett says. "If you let the rig drag behind the boat, you will hang up continuously. Use your trolling motor to control the speed of your drift," he advises, "and let out line as the hole deepens. Keep bouncing the big sinker off of the bottom; pick it up a few feet and then lower it back to the bottom."

Collett prefers a heavy 7½-foot flippin-stick and a sturdy baitcasting reel spooled with 20- to 25-pound mono. The long rod gives him the extra leverage he needs to pull big blues out of their rocky haunts. His terminal tackle consists of a 2-ounce bell sinker tied to the end of his line and an exquisitely sharp 1/0 hook attached to a loop in the line (p. 65) about a foot above the sinker. With this rig, the sinker stays in contact with the bottom but the bait is slightly elevated, and you can change hooks quickly should the need arise.

Shad is the predominant forage in the Tennessee River, so Collett's favorite bait is either whole shad or shad parts.

"To catch numbers of catfish, the best bait that I know of is shad guts, with cut pieces of shad running a close second," he says.

"Chicken liver is also a productive bait, but when I'm looking for big fish, I like to use whole shad (live or dead) about 4 to 6 inches long, or half of an even bigger shad."

Though some might think a 1/0 hook is too small, Collett deems it necessary in order to get a good hookset in deep water. "Because monofilament stretches, it is hard to drive a thick hook into a catfish's tough mouth when you are working 50 feet or more

beneath the boat," Collett says. "A smaller hook that is honed needle-sharp will penetrate much better, and I think a quality 1/0 hook is strong enough to hold a giant cat if you play him correctly."

Because of the jagged rocks found in the best cat holes, it's important to pull the fish off bottom in a hurry. That's why Collett uses a stout baitcasting outfit with 30-pound mono. "When a fish strikes, you need to set the hook very hard and try to get the fish moving upward as quickly as possible," Collett points out. "If you don't get him off of the bottom in just a few seconds, he will either cut your line on a rock or tangle you up."

Holmes's Method

Like Collett, Holmes employs a drifting, bottom bouncing technique. Using his depthfinder to keep the boat positioned directly over the river channel bank, he drifts with the current while bouncing his bait slowly off the bottom. "I use the trolling motor only to keep the boat over the top of the structure, and to move the boat slightly so that I keep my bait directly under the boat," he explains. Depending on the particular dog-leg, Holmes's drift might be as short as 100 yards or as long as half a mile.

"I prefer using this technique in rivers because I believe the current concentrates the fish," Holmes says. "This same technique will work in reservoirs; the only difference is that you use your trolling motor to ease the boat along the side of the river channel."

Because Holmes's passion is channel cats, which run

considerably smaller than the blues Collett pursues, he can get by with lighter tackle, usually a medium-power bass outfit spooled with 15-pound mono.

Holmes's all-time favorite catfish bait is a fresh catalpa worm, but he also uses shad guts, cut river herring and nightcrawlers (because they're convenient). But catalpa worms are available for only a few weeks each year, so he freezes them for later use. He boils them for about 20 seconds, lets them cool and then freezes them in water. This method retains their texture and color.

Holmes's bottom-fishing rig is much like Collett's, though down-sized slightly with a 3/4- to 1-ounce sinker and a size 2 to 1/0 hook. But Holmes makes a slight, but important, modification to the rig, slipping a 1/2-inch piece of plastic worm onto the hook so it covers the hook eye.

"I do this to add a little buoyancy to the bait," he says, "but I also think that a little bit of color will often attract the fish to your bait." Holmes prefers red, but also uses blue, black and chartreuse. "I have seen instances where that little piece of worm made all the difference in the world, so I now use it all of the time."

How to Make a Bottom-Bouncer Rig

1 Tie a double surgeon's loop about a foot from the end of your line by **(a)** doubling the line and forming a loop, **(b)** passing the doubled line through the loop twice and **(c)** snugging up the knot.

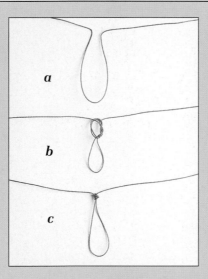

2 Attach the hook by threading the loop through the eye, bringing the hook point through the loop and then pulling on the hook to snug up the connection.

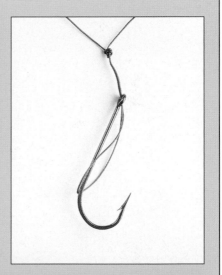

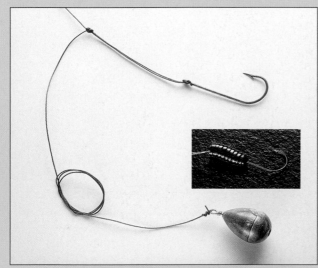

3 Complete the rig by tying a 3/4- to 2-ounce bell sinker to the end of the line. If desired, slip a 1/2-inch piece of plastic worm over the hook eye to add buoyancy and a touch of color (inset).

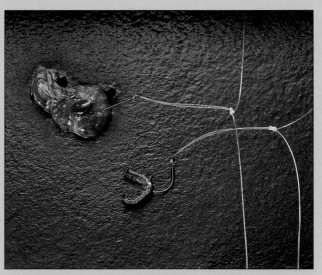

4 Hook shad guts by pushing them over the hook point several times (top), just as you would gob on a nightcrawler. Hook a catalpa worm through the back as shown (bottom).

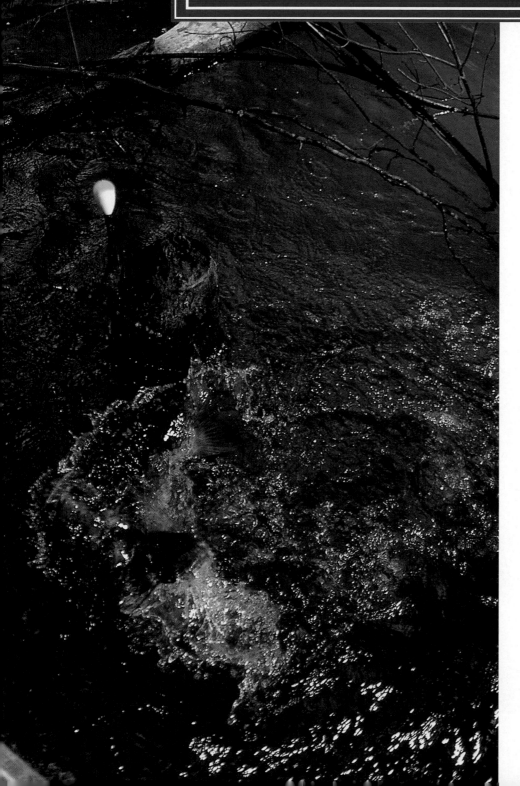

OUT OF THE ORDINARY

S ome of the very best catfishing takes place at times or in places the average angler never even considers.

NIGHTTIME CATS

by Clark Montgomery

Night fishing for cats is a long-standing tradition throughout the South and is rapidly catching on among northcountry anglers. And for good reason: Chances are you'll catch more cats than you ever dreamed possible, and your odds of tangling with a monster fish are much greater than they are in daylight hours.

Jim Moyer, Dixie's premier catman and a frequent night fisherman, explains why the method is so effective: "Catfish have poor vision compared to other predators like bass or crappie, so to compensate, they've developed tremendous senses of smell, taste and hearing.

Research has shown that a catfish can smell its food 60 feet away. Besides, catfish often live in turbid or muddy water, so even during the daytime there may be little light penetration in their world. No wonder night feeding comes natural to them."

Of the various catfish species, the most nocturnal is the flathead. "These fish are real night stalkers," Moyer notes. "They often hole up in logjams or along undercut banks during the day and emerge at night to feed.

Channel and blue cats, on the other hand, will feed actively both day and night."

Moyer has caught enormous cats of each species, but admits that his passion is giant blues. He's boated hundreds of blue cats weighing in excess of 35 pounds; the biggest to date is a hulking 87-pounder. Some 40 percent of these monsters were caught at night.

Moyer prefers to night-fish on "river-run" reservoirs, such as Lake Barkley, a 124-mile-long impoundment on the Cumberland River in Kentucky and Tennessee. This type of reservoir has a relatively narrow channel and noticeable current which, according to Moyer, activates the catfish bite.

Some of the information presented here is specific to impoundments of this type, but most can be applied to any kind of man-made lake.

Jim Moyer displays a giant nighttime blue.

Lake Barkley, with its narrow basin and noticeable current, is a typical river-run reservoir.

WHEN & WHERE

Although most catmen do their night fishing during the summer months, Moyer maintains it's a year-round proposition.

In a river-run reservoir, current is an often-overlooked factor that has a dramatic effect on catfish location. "I've found if there's no current in a river-run reservoir, I might as well stay home," Moyer says. "Catfish bite remarkably well at night in 5 to 15 feet of water when the lake or river is rising—it brings them out of their deeper haunts."

A rise may also muddy up the water, which Moyer says is good. "I love muddy water, day or night. It's perfect when it's the color of a cup of coffee with one cream in it." Always call the dam office before your trip and ask about the generating schedule.

Here's where Moyer finds the fish in each season:

Spring

"In a river-run reservoir, check out the headwaters (upper end) of the lake as the water warms," Moyer advises. "Cats often make a spawning run toward the upstream dam. Always target heavy cover in the spring, no matter what depth zone you're fishing. Flatheads will spawn around shallow rocks and sunken logs in tributaries with little current flow; channels and blues will be on deep ledges with a strong current flow. Now is the time to move often, testing both deep and shallow water, since cats can be from 2 to 50 feet deep depending on their species and mood."

"Flatheads and channel cats can tolerate much warmer water than blues. Since I mainly target big blues, I fish a lot of deep water at night in the early spring and winter; these fish

get really active when the water is between 36 and 39°F."

Summer

"Most fishermen think of catfish as being bottom-oriented," Moyer points out, "but I believe many of the biggest cats suspend over the thermocline in the summer, both day and night. This is especially true with blues, which may go dormant in warm water and suspend to conserve energy. They often hang over treetops and river channel structure."

Moyer has seen some unusual patterns take shape at night after the spawn. Easily the weirdest is flatheads schooling on the surface, a phenomenon he has witnessed several times. "The first time I saw this, I was coming in from a bass fishing trip on Lake Barkley right at dark and noticed some big fish, presumably stripers, schooling on top. I pulled closer to investigate and was astounded to see they were huge flathead cats busting shad—some of these fish were over 60 pounds! I tried catching them on a topwater plug, but they wouldn't hit it. Since then I've seen flatheads surfacing on other occasions, always right before dark and always in May, but I have yet to catch any. Probably the best technique would be to cast a live baitfish on a float into the school."

Fall

Once the water drops to 65°F, big cats come alive on main-lake structure at night. Look for them on deep, fast-sloping ledges.

Current can be the determining factor now, particularly when you're targeting blues. Current flow may be neither as frequent nor as intense as in summer and winter, when power demands are greater, so timing is especially important.

Winter

This is Moyer's favorite time to night-fish cats. He focuses primarily on deep ledges in the main river channel, especially those that have a series of stair-step ledges rather than a smooth, sharp break.

"Flatheads are very hard to catch now, but channels and blues will bite all winter long," he says. "Winter is prime time for the biggest blues, which crave cold water. I've caught blues to 70 pounds at night when the water temp was only 36°F. Current is usually crankin' now due to frequent winter rains and high power demands."

Seasonal Locations in River-Run Reservoirs

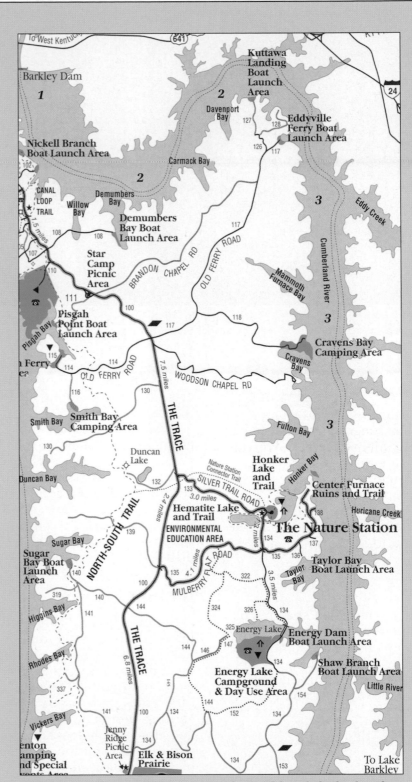

In a river-run reservoir such as Lake Barkley, fish the headwaters toward the upstream dam (1) as the water warms in spring. Look for suspended blues around river channel structure (2) in summer. Hit deep ledges and structure, often in the main lake (3) in fall and winter.

Float fishing is one essential part of an effective night-fishing repertoire.

NIGHT-FISHING TECHNIQUES

Moyer employs a variety of night-fishing methods, depending on the season and the type of water. Here are some of his favorites.

Float Fishing

During the pre-spawn period, Moyer's favorite technique is float fishing along the shallow rocky banks where cats often spawn. His primary targets at this time are channel cats, so he can get by with spinning tackle. Using a stiff spinning outfit spooled with 10-pound mono, he baits up with a live minnow or bluegill and sets the float to keep the bait at a depth of 2 to 5 feet. Then he slowly works his way down the bank with his trolling motor or simply drifts with the current, letting his bait bump the rocks.

"It's not a big-fish method," he says, "but it's great for keeper-size fish. One night I caught 150 [channel] cats from 1 to 8 pounds using this technique."

In summer, Moyer often catches suspended blues on a slip-bobber rig baited with a chunk of freshly caught skipjack. He puts out a couple of rods with floats set to fish 20 feet down over a 60-foot channel and just lets the boat drift with the current.

Bottom Fishing

In fall, when cats are holding on deep, fast-sloping ledges, Moyer anchors up and sets out three lines to cover a variety of depths. "Stagger three lines with cut bait at various depths down to 45 feet along the ledge," he advises. "It's not unusual to pick up a flathead on the shallowest rod, a channel cat on the middle rod and a big blue on the deep rod."

Moyer normally relies on a slip-sinker rig with a heavy weight, but when he's having trouble getting his bait to stay put in the current, he may switch to a 3-way rig with a pyramid sinker (p. 73).

Because there's a chance of catching a giant blue on any of these lines, Moyer uses a beefy 7 to 7½-foot Berkley E-Cat rod (his own design) combined with an Ambassadeur 7000 reel spooled with 40- to 50-pound mono.

Common Mistakes

Night fishermen can greatly increase their success by avoiding some common mistakes, Moyer believes. The most frequent errors include:

•**Staying in one spot too long.** "Catfish aren't tentative feeders at night, Moyer says. "They're usually hungry and aggressive. If you're using the right bait, it should get eaten —if there are any fish in the area. I see too many catfishermen sticking on one spot all night long, usually a place where they caught some good fish in the past. But catfish are roamers. They hunt baitfish at night; no bait, no cats. If I don't see some action in 30 minutes, I move."

•**Fishing the wrong depth zone.** Moyer finds cats in an amazingly broad range of depths at night, depending on species, water temperature and season. "Flatheads may move so shallow at night they'll hit a bass lure," he maintains. "I've caught big ones on plastic worms and jigs in 18 inches of water. Channels occasionally move very shallow as well, but they're usually deeper than flatheads at night."

But the deepest cats of all, Moyer has found, are the giant blues. "I routinely fish them in the 30- to 45-foot zone. They will occasionally move into shallow water, especially when spawning, but year-round, this is the best depth range for a big blue. If you're fishing a spot you feel ought to hold cats, but aren't catching any, try moving deeper or shallower on the structure."

• **Using "stinkbaits."** This limits your chances of encountering a giant cat, Moyer believes. "I am absolutely convinced that the biggest cats prefer real food. Stinkbaits have their place, but they're typically most effec-tive on smaller fish. Some of these concoctions, especially the pastes, are better suited to still water than current."

Moyer's experience shows cats in excess of 20 pounds respond better to fish baits than crawlers or redworms at night. "Live shiners or creek minnows work great after dark for all catfish species. Live bluegills, where legal, are awesome at night for flatheads." Another good night-fishing bait, albeit an expensive one, is shrimp; Spam can also work.

But for a monster cat, Moyer says that nothing can top chunks or filets of fresh skipjack (river herring) fished on the bottom. Obsessive about his bait, Moyer uses a light spinning outfit with a pair of ⅛-ounce white twister-tail grubs to catch his skipjack immediately before a catfish outing. "The skipjack is an extremely oily and aro-matic fish, and if there's a cat in the area, he'll find it," Moyer insists.

Night-Fishing Rigs

Slip-Sinker Rig. Thread a 3-ounce egg sinker onto your line, add a large barrel swivel, then tie on a 2-foot leader and a size 6/0 to 9/0 "Octopus"-style hook.

Lighted Slip-Float Rig. Tie a slip-bobber knot onto your line, add a bead and then thread your line through the small hole at the bottom of the float. Then add a Rubber-Cor sinker and a hook (size depends on type of bait). This type of float is powered by a tiny lithium battery.

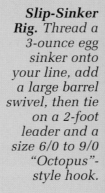

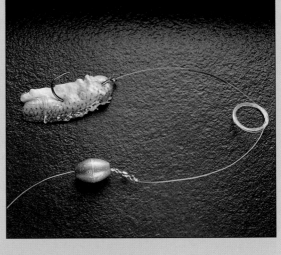

3-Way Rig. Tie a large 3-way swivel to the end of your line, add a 2-foot leader and a hook and then a 1-foot dropper and a flat-bottomed, pyramid-style sinker (about 3 ounces). A pyra-mid, unlike an egg sinker, will not roll in the current.

Barkley Dam

Releases

Date	Time	Units
12/11/2000	6am - midnight (CT)	1

Observed

Date	Upstream Elevation (feet above mean sea level)	Downstream Elevation (feet above mean sea level)	Average Hourly* Discharge (cubic feet per second)
12/10/2000 11pm (CT)	354.55	302.95	9,000
12/10/2000 12 midnight (CT)	354.55	302.95	9,000
12/11/2000 1am (CT)	354.65	303.15	9,000
12/11/2000 2am (CT)	354.65	303.15	9,000
12/11/2000 3am (CT)	354.70	303.20	9,000
12/11/2000 4am (CT)	354.70	303.20	9,000
12/11/2000 5am (CT)	354.75	303.25	9,000
12/11/2000 6am (CT)	354.75	303.25	9,000

* discharge reported at end of hour

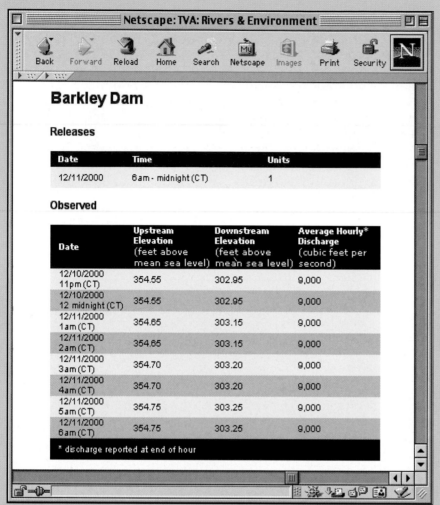

Information on water level and discharge rate is critical in fishing a river-run reservoir. For TVA lakes such as Barkley, this data can be obtained at the TVA website (www.lakeinfo.tva.gov). You can also get the information by calling the dam office.

Set your anchor on a towel or rubber mat so it doesn't bang on the floor of the boat. Catfish are extremely sensitive to noise at night.

Keep your boat's decks and floor clear of obstructions like anchor ropes, extra rods, etc. When you hook a big cat, you'll need plenty of room to maneuver and you don't want to trip over your gear.

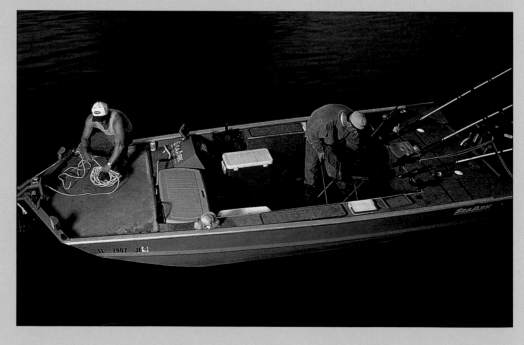

When cats are shallow in spring, they can be easily spooked if you shine a bright light on the water. Wear a headlamp and use it only when necessary.

To make your line more visible at night, spool up with fluorescent mono and illuminate it with a black light attached to your gunwale.

If your bottom-fishing rigs aren't producing, try rigging your bait to fish higher. Catfish often "feed up" at night and if your bait is too close to the bottom, they may ignore it. To lift the bait farther off bottom, use a 3-way rig with a longer-than-normal dropper or attach a float to your leader.

BREAKTHROUGH FOR WINTER FLATHEADS

by Dick Sternberg with Chris Winchester

"**F**latheads don't bite in the winter— period!!!"

That was my terse reaction when Chris Winchester told me he'd been hearing rumors of some anglers catching big flatheads on the Mississippi River in January.

And he wasn't talking about Louisiana waters of the Mississippi. He was referring to the Minnesota-Wisconsin boundary waters, where you have to dodge floating ice

chunks if you want to fish that time of the year.

Winchester, who is rapidly gaining a reputation as one of the river's top catfish guides, is a credible kind of guy. He has a 2-inch-thick scrapbook loaded with Polaroid photos of himself and his clients hoisting 40- to 60-pound flatheads, but most of these fish were caught in summer and fall. Like most catmen, he has always believed that flatheads

Chris Winchester displays a 40-pound-plus winter flathead.

don't bite in cold water.

I tend to believe most of what Winchester tells me, but I just couldn't buy the winter flathead story. "Are the fish actually biting or are they snagging them?" I asked.

"From what I hear, they're catching the fish on big jigs—and most of them are hooked in the mouth," he replied.

There was good reason for my skepticism: While working as a fisheries biologist for the Minnesota DNR three decades ago, I collected thousands of catfish (flatheads and channels) with gillnets, hoopnets, slat traps, trawls and shocking boats for the purpose of tagging them and studying their movements.

One notable finding of the research was that there were several very specific catfish wintering spots in the study area. Lots of anglers knew about these areas (even before the study) and were catching scads of cats through the ice each winter.

That probably sounds like a confirmation of what Winchester was saying, but there was one problem: All of these fish were illegally snagged!

After a few fishermen were tagged for snagging, a controversy began to develop. Anglers argued that snagging should be legalized because catfish were a "commercial" species and large numbers of them were being netted from the wintering holes. Since the fish were dormant in winter, anglers maintained, there was no way of getting them to bite. Snagging was the only way anglers could get their "fair share."

The DNR eventually gave in to the public outcry and a wintertime snagging season was established in 1979. But

Groups of winter catfish snaggers on Minnesota-Wisconsin waters of Mississippi River circa 1970.

the snagging ban was reinstated in 1990.

Despite my certainty that the flatheads were being snagged, I continued to hear reports from Winchester and others that the fish were indeed biting. One night, Chris called with another update. "That's it," he said in a disgusted tone. "They slaughtered 'em again today. I can't stand it anymore—I'm heading for the river tomorrow to get this thing figured out."

"Keep me posted," I said. I'll believe it when I see it with my own eyes."

Chris wasted no time in convincing me I was wrong. His tone of voice was a lot more upbeat in the next night's phone call. "You won't believe it, but I caught 35 flatheads today," he began. "Some of them were snagged, but some hit really hard. Biggest was 50 pounds—and he was hooked right in the mouth."

All good wintering spots have one thing in common: lots of cover to break the current.

FINDING WINTER FLATHEADS

It would be nice if there were a definite set of conditions that determined where flatheads spend the winter. Lots of writers refer to the "deep wintering holes," implying that the fish congregate in washout holes, deep bends, etc. But that's simply not the case.

Here are some examples of spots on the Mississippi where large numbers of flathead and channel catfish concentrate during the winter months.

• A straight stretch of the main channel with moderate current and a depth of 15 to 20 feet.

• A 25- to 35-foot washout hole below a wing dam.

• A 15- to 25-foot flat off the mouth of a major tributary.

• A 65-foot hole at the foot of a river lake, where the current speeds up as it funnels through the narrowing channel.

• A 30-foot hole near the upstream end of a long rock pile in a river lake.

Although none of these spots bears much resemblance to any of the others, nearly all of them have one feature in common: Lots of heavy cover in the form of rocks, logs and branches, but sometimes large rocks.

Photographer Doug Stamm's observations (sidebar, p. 79) definitely confirmed the importance of cover. The catfish area was exposed to a moderate current, and practically every fish was in the "soft spot" below a rock, log or branch. Many cats were resting behind surprisingly small branches—only a few inches in diameter. Evidently they provide an adequate cur-rent break. All of the fish were resting right on the bottom, where the current is weakest.

By now you're probably thinking, "This is all pretty interesting, but how can I locate one of these winter catfish hot spots?"

If you're fishing a river where other anglers have already done the research, you might be able to tap in to that knowledge by inquiring of local sources like bait-shop operators, conservation officers, state fisheries personnel or anglers who spend a lot of time on the river.

Figuring it out for yourself won't be easy because there are no visual signs to tip you off, and you probably won't be able to see the fish on your depthfinder because of their bottom-hugging habits.

You may, however, be able

to see the boulders, logs and branches that the fish use for cover, and your depth finder may occasionally reveal a "mound" of fish stacked on the bottom (p. 84).

Don't expect to find cats on every rock pile or in every tangle of woody cover. For reasons that only the fish know, they will select a certain spot and ignore a dozen others that seem nearly identical.

The bottom line is this: If you really want to find a winter cat hole in an unfamiliar river, you'll have to grab a rod and reel and go out and fish for them. That won't be easy but, with so many cats concentrated in such a small area, you normally don't have to "wait them out." If you don't hook up in one or two drifts through a likely spot, move on to the next one.

Once you find a spot that holds a good number of cats, note the precise location. Most cat concentrations are close to shore, so that shouldn't be a problem. Chances are, the fish will be in exactly the same spot in future years, assuming the cover hasn't been washed out by a flood.

That's exactly what happened in one of the spots where Stamm made his catfish count back in the 70s. After several major spring floods in the past two decades, the spot now has much less woody cover and holds only a small fraction of the cats it once did. Now, the fish have moved to another spot across the river—a spot with a cluttered mess of woody cover on the bottom.

Best Times

Catfish begin moving into their wintering areas in late fall, when the water temperature drops below 40°F. The concentration builds until the water temperature is near freezing. The fish remain in the same area through winter but, once the water temperature rises to the upper 30s in spring, they start to disperse. Rising water in spring also scatters the fish.

Winchester has found that fishing is best on warm, sunny days. "The fish are more active and fight much better in warm weather," he says.

Swimming with the Cats *by Dick Sternberg*

Back in the early 70s, while vertically jigging for Mississippi River walleyes in early spring, I stumbled upon a new flathead spot. On several occasions, I accidentally snagged giant cats while drifting along the same rocky section of the main channel.

I suspected it was a wintering area, so I contacted Doug Stamm, now one of the country's top underwater photographers. At the time, Doug was working with the Sea Grant Program at the University of Wisconsin, and took great interest in what I was telling him. He agreed to meet me and my DNR crew for a day on the river to scout the catfish concentration.

Wearing Scuba gear, Doug swam through the catfish hole, taking dozens of photos with an underwater camera. At one point, he grabbed a 20-pound flathead and brought it up to the surface for us to see. The fish had a heavy layer of silt on its back and made little effort to escape. Doug estimated that there were more than 1,000 catfish in an area about 50 feet wide and 500 feet long.

A few years later, divers conducted a more formal survey of several known catfish concentrations. Swimming designated transects, counting the fish and then extrapolating to determine the total number of fish in the area led to an estimate of 2,350 catfish per acre in the area of densest concentration.

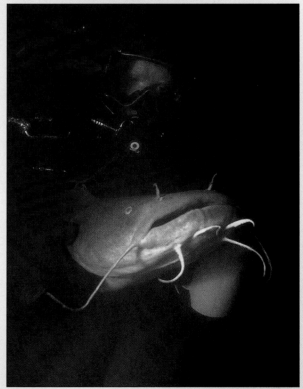

Wintering catfish are often so dormant that divers can grab them and carry them to the surface.

Prime Winter Catfish Locations

This straight stretch of rocky shoreline along the main channel is a major wintering area, even though there are no visual clues to its existence.

Winter catfish congregate in eddies around submerged wing dams.

In this widening of the Mississippi River, the upstream lip of a long rock pile (left) and a deep hole in the narrows at the foot of the lake (dotted line, right) are known catfish wintering areas.

Catfish often nestle between logs that break the current.

A channel cat (right) uses a larger flathead (left) as a current break.

A flathead wedged between a pair of rocks.

Wintering cats may be so dormant that a layer of silt accumulates on their back (fish in foreground).

CATCHING WINTER FLATHEADS

In the majority of large rivers, even those in the north country, the main channel remains ice-free through most of the winter. Thin ice may form after a week of sub-zero temperatures, but rarely will there be enough to allow ice fishing. Practically all winter flatheads are caught by drifting and vertically jigging in open water.

The Gear

Winchester believes in beefy gear. His favorite jigging outfit consists of a 7-foot muskie rod and an Ambassadeur 6500 baitcasting reel spooled with 80-pound superline (his favorite is Berkley Whiplash). He doesn't like mono because it is too stiff and springy in cold weather.

The hooks on ordinary jig heads are too small and flimsy, so Winchester uses 1- to 3-ounce saltwater jigs with heavy size 6/0-7/0 hooks. He tips them with 5- to 6-inch soft-plastic shad, curlytails or tube-style trailers. When fishing is slow, he may add a 4- to 5-inch shiner for scent appeal.

The Jigging Method

Once you've found the right spot, the rest is easy. Just lower your jig to the bottom and work it very slowly, lifting it no more than a foot and then letting it drop.

"At first, I was working my jig way too hard," Winchester recalls. "I was snagging some

To detect light strikes and minimize snagging, it's important to keep your line near vertical.

Jigs for Winter Flatheads

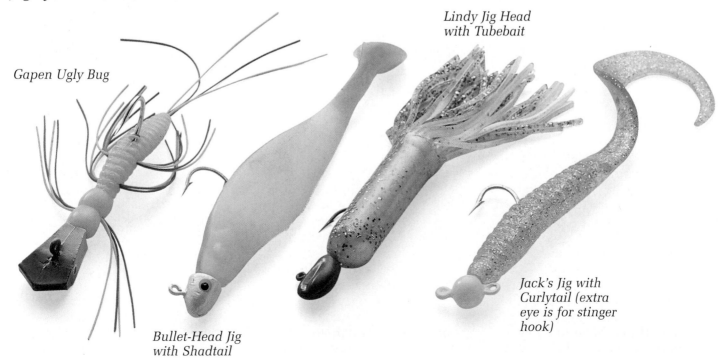

Gapen Ugly Bug

Lindy Jig Head with Tubebait

Bullet-Head Jig with Shadtail

Jack's Jig with Curlytail (extra eye is for stinger hook)

Drift-Jigging for Winter Flatheads

1 *Lower your jig to the bottom and begin jigging it slowly as your boat drifts with the current. Watch your line angle closely; if it stays near vertical, no adjustment is necessary. But if it starts to angle away from the boat (shown), you'll have to adjust your drift speed with your trolling motor.*

2 *Run your trolling motor in the direction in which the line is trailing. In this example, the line is trailing upstream, so the angler trolls in an upstream direction to bring the line back to vertical.*

big cats, but very few were actually hitting the jig. I knew there had to be lots of fish in the area, so I just kept experimenting to find the right presentation. Sometimes the best action is practically no action at all."

A slow jigging action also minimizes hang-ups. If you rip your jig up and down, you'll eventually sink the hook into a log—and you probably won't be able to pull it out. Even with a gentle jigging stroke, snags are a fact of life. In fact, if you're not getting snagged, you're not fishing the right kind of water. You'll just have to carry a good supply of jigs.

While drifting, it's important to keep your line as close to vertical as possible. If you let it trail at an angle, you'll be snagged constantly. The trick is to keep your boat drifting at *exactly* the speed of the current.

In order to do that, you'll have to compensate for the wind. For example, if the wind is blowing downstream, you'll have to point your trolling motor upstream to compensate. With an upstream wind, you'll have to troll downstream. The idea is to troll in the direction your line is trailing until it becomes vertical, and then maintain the speed necessary

to keep it there.

"Every once in a while, you'll feel a solid rap," Winchester notes, "but most of the time you'll just feel a little weight. When you feel anything out of the ordinary, always set the hook."

When conditions are right, you'll catch an astounding number of cats. "On a good day, I'll land 30 to 40," Winchester says, "and at least one will go 40-plus pounds. So far, my biggest winter flathead is 58. But the other day, I fought one for half an hour before he bent my hook and got off. I've taken flatheads over 60 pounds in the summer, and this one was a lot bigger."

Look for "mounds" of catfish on your depth finder. Occasionally, you'll see a hump on the bottom that could be a group of fish stacked up vertically. When you lower your jig, you'll feel it bumping down through the fish.

When the action is slow, squirt some bottled scent (preferably baitfish flavor) onto your jig. Or tip your jig with a minnow or piece of cut bait for additional scent appeal.

Winter Flathead Ethics

While there's no doubt that some flatheads continue to feed during the wintering period, many of them are absolutely dormant. Divers note that some of the fish have heavy silt deposits on their back, indicating a long period of inactivity.

In the short time that Mississippi River catfish guide Chris Winchester has been studying the habits of winter flatheads, he has found that the fish are much more active in late fall and early winter than they are in midwinter. "Seems like they're much more aggressive when the water temperature is at least 40°F, " he says. "When it's down in the mid-30s, I have a hard time getting them to bite. In fact, I quit fishing for them this past February, because practically all of the fish were snagged."

Winchester suspects that the fish will start biting again when the water warms to 40°F

in spring, but he has yet to study them during the spring period, so he doesn't know for sure.

Compared to fish that have scales, catfish are very easy to snag. The hook point doesn't deflect, it

just sinks in. "I worry about what might happen if the wrong group of guys found one of these winter concentrations," Winchester said with a pained expression. "If they wanted to keep all the catfish they snagged, they could wipe out the whole wintering concentration in a few days."

Even if the fish are caught legally, catch-and-release is of utmost importance if you plan on pursuing winter flatheads. "When the fish are concentrated that tightly, they're extremely vulnerable," Winchester notes. "Catfish from a long stretch of river are stacked into an area not much bigger than your living room. If those fish were removed, summertime catfish action would suffer for years, maybe forever."

Catch-and-release is a must when fishing a winter flathead concentration. Good fishing ethics allow no other option!

Flatheads through the Ice

If the catfish river you fish freezes solid in winter, there's a good chance you can still catch flatheads, if you know where they concentrate in late fall. Once they set up in their wintering areas, they're not likely to move until spring. If you don't know where the fish hole up, the odds are against you. The wintering spots are tough enough to find in open water, let alone when ice limits your mobility.

But if you know right where they are, fishing through the ice can be even more effective than fishing in open water because you can stay right on top of the fish 100 percent of the time.

One of the biggest problems you'll face is cutting a hole big enough for a giant flathead. Even a 10-inch ice auger (the largest available) won't cut a hole large enough for a 50-pound flathead. There are two solutions: Cut a triangle of three closely spaced holes and chisel out the bridges with a heavy ice spud, or cut a large hole using a

chain saw. The latter method is much easier.

If you don't mind standing up, you can use the same gear as you would for open-water fishing. But if you like to fish sitting down, you'll want a stout jigging rod from 3½ to 4 feet long. You probably won't be able to find a factory-made rod that's stiff enough, but you can easily make your own by adding a tip top to an old broken rod. Pair it with a baitcasting reel spooled with 30- to 50-pound superline, and you're ready to go.

Because you don't have to worry about keeping your line vertical as you do in open water, you can get by with a much lighter jig, from 3/8 to 5/8 ounce. But be sure to use a jig with a heavy hook, such as a bass jig or a salt-water jig. Instead of

tipping it with a soft-plastic trailer, use a 3- to 4-inch minnow. Work the jig the same way you would if fishing in open water.

Whenever you venture out on a frozen river, be sure to carry a heavy, sharp chisel to test the ice thickness. Walk slowly, giving the ice a couple of good whacks after each step. Never attempt to drive your car on river ice and always carry a set of ice picks to help you crawl out should you fall through.

Cut an 18- to 24-inch-diameter hole using a chain saw, then cut the block into smaller pieces that can easily be removed from the water. When you're done fishing, mark the hole well so someone else doesn't fall in.

Secrets of the Catfish Pros

DOG-DAYS CATS

by Chris Altman

It was a brutally hot August, as I remember it. School was scheduled to start in a few weeks and, until that dreaded day, I was determined to spend every available minute at the pond.

It was a great fishing spot for a 12-year-old—full of channel cats and just a short Schwinn-ride away from home. Armed with my best rig—a solid-glass rod and a trusty Zebco 33 that I'd bought with my grass-mowing money—I would leave home at daybreak, stopping along the way to collect minnows and crayfish from the traps set in a nearby creek.

I had caught enough cats through the summer to keep me entertained and had my line broken often enough to convince me that there were some monster catfish just waiting for my offering.

But in August, the cats seemed to disappear. After several days without so much as a nibble, frustration was setting in. One day, an old man joined me on the shore and, after rigging his bait beneath a large balsa wood float, began catching catfish as fast as he could toss the rig into the water. And still, my bait remained unmolested on the bottom of the lake.

Perplexed and curious, I asked the veteran angler about his technique. "You gotta pull your bait off the bottom when the water gets hot," he said. "Don't know why, but it's the only way to catch 'em."

We finagled a trade: one of his bobbers for the five crayfish I had in my battered minnow bucket. After he showed me how to rig the float so it would suspend the bait about 8 feet deep, I began catching fish.

For many years, I never understood why the old man's advice helped me catch so many hot-weather catfish. But as my fishing world broadened and I began plying a variety of larger lakes, I found that his advice had merit in those waters as well. The method is effective not only for channel cats, but for blues as well.

Here's why the old man's system works so well and how you can apply it to the waters you fish.

The lessons learned as a child may last a lifetime.

WHY CATS SUSPEND IN SUMMER

In summer, most lakes that support catfish stratify into three distinct temperature layers: the upper layer, or *epilimnion;* the middle layer, or *metalimnion*; and the lower layer, or *hypolimnion.*

Water in the epilimnion is warmer and thus lighter than that in the metalimnion and, as a result of the density difference, is easily circulated by the wind. Any water below the epilimnion resists mixing. As a result, the epilimnion stays uniformly warm and well oxygenated, while the temperature and oxygen level drops through the metalimnion. The part of the metalimnion where the temperature drops fastest is called the *thermocline.* The hypolimnion has the coldest water and lowest oxygen level.

Because of this stratification, the vertical movements of catfish are restricted by the oxygen barrier. In most lakes, you'll find the greatest number of catfish in or just above the thermocline. Although the precise level where you find the fish varies depending on the type of lake, they're most commonly at depths of 12 to 25 feet.

As the surface water begins to cool in early fall, it gets denser than the warmer water below, causing it to sink. The surface water keeps cooling and sinking until the entire lake is the same temperature from top to bottom. This phenomenon is known as the *fall turnover.* With the density of the water now equalized, even a light wind causes all of the water in the lake to mix, removing the oxygen barrier and allowing catfish to swim at any depth they choose.

The turnover takes place at different times, even on adjacent lakes, depending on the shape of the lake basin. All other factors being equal, a deep lake turns over later than a shallow one. The depths are much colder in a deep lake, and it takes longer for the surface water to cool enough to match the temperature in the depths.

The implications for anglers are obvious: If you want to catch cats during the dog days of summer, you must keep your bait in the depth range to which the fish are restricted. That doesn't necessarily mean that you can't fish your bait on the bottom, but it does mean that you can fish no deeper than the limit of adequate dissolved oxygen (below).

Where to Find Catfish in a Stratified Lake

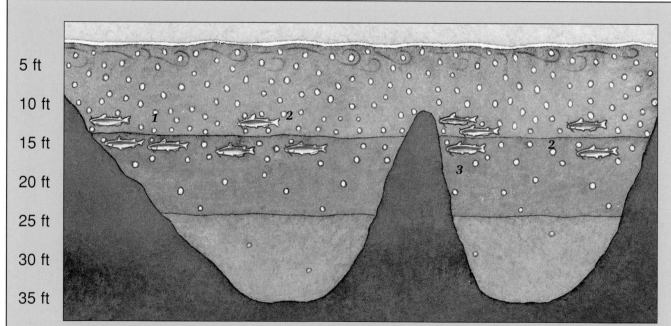

In this hypothetical lake, which has a maximum depth of 35 feet, the thermocline forms at a depth of 15 to 25 feet. The catfish usually suspend just above the thermocline or in the upper portion of it; you'll find most them at 12 to 17 feet in the following areas: **(1)** *along a gradual shoreline break,* **(2)** *suspended in open water and* **(3)** *around the peak of a midlake hump that intersects the thermocline.*

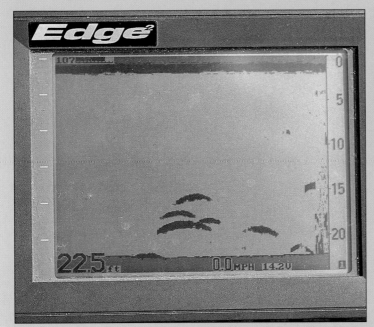

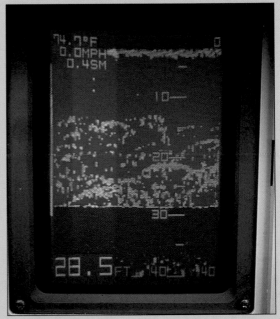

A graph with good resolution can help you find suspended catfish in 2 ways: You can motor around the lake and look for a layer of suspended fish (left) or, if you can't find the fish, you can use your graph to look for the layer of plankton that often collects in the thermocline (right). In order to see the band, however, you'll probably have to turn up the "gain" or sensitivity of your unit. Chances are, you'll find catfish in or just above the upper limits of the plankton band.

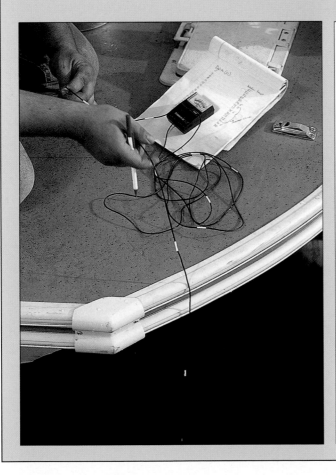

Depth (ft)	Water Temp.	
2	82	
4	80	
6	80	
8	80	
10	80	
12	79.5	
14	78.5	⎫
16	77	
18	75.5	
20	74	Thermocline
22	73	
24	72	
26	71	⎭
28	70.5	
30	70	
32	69.5	
34	69	
36	68.5	

Stop over deep water and then slowly lower the probe of an electric thermometer with a metered cord (far left). The temperature will remain almost constant until the probe reaches the upper limit of the thermocline; then the temperature will drop at a rate of approximately .5°F per foot until it exits the lower limit of the thermocline; then the temperature will continue to drop, but at a much slower rate. To determine the limits of the thermocline, plot the temperature at 2-foot intervals and identify the zone where the temperature drops at least .5°F per foot (left). In this example, the thermocline has formed at 14 to 26 feet.

Carl Lowrance, 1913-1995.

HOW TO CATCH DOG-DAYS CATS

"I have seen acres and acres of catfish suspended right on top of the thermocline. You can see them on a depth finder of any sort, and it is a breathtaking experience. People just don't realize how many catfish are in our lakes."

– Carl Lowrance—Founder of Lowrance Electronics, 1982

Carl Lowrance discovered dog-days cats decades ago and, once he retired from the electronics business, spent a good deal of his time catching cats suspended over open water. His favorite method was jug fishing, which in fact may be the best way to catch these fish.

"Since the catfish are as apt to be suspended in the middle of the lake as they are around the shoreline," Lowrance reasoned, "I wanted a technique that would cover a lot of water for me, and jug fishing seemed to be perfect."

Other Options

If you're like most anglers, you prefer catching cats on a rod and reel to chasing a bunch of jugs around the lake. Here are the best "hands-on" methods for catching cats suspended in a specific layer of water:

Slip-Float Fishing. This is a good choice when you have a pretty good idea of where to find the fish. Let's say you've done some scouting with your depth finder and found a school of cats suspended in open water, far from any kind of structure or cover. Or, maybe you've located some cats holding on a piece of structure, such as a mid-lake hump. Then all you have to do is toss out a marker, anchor your boat just upwind of the school and then rig a slip-float outfit to keep your bait in the upper portion of the fish zone.

As long as the fish stay put, you'll enjoy nonstop action. That's a lot more likely if the fish are relating to structure than if they're out in the middle of nowhere. If the action slows, be prepared to go on another scouting run. Often, cats suspended in open water don't go far; you may find them within 50 or 100 yards of the spot where you found them originally.

Drifting. Let's say you find some cats suspended over an open area of the lake, but they're scattered rather than tightly concentrated. In this situation, you might catch a fish or two by anchoring up and tossing out a slip-float, but your coverage will be limited.

If you like watching a float, you could just toss out a slip-float rig and let your boat drift through the fish zone. But you may have trouble setting the hook with a float drifting far from your boat. That's why many savvy catmen prefer to drift-fish without the float. Just lower your sinker and bait so it fishes right below the boat as it drifts through the fish zone.

If you're using a single rod, it's a good idea to hold onto it; that way, you can set the hook immediately when you feel a bite. But if you're fishing with several rods, set them in rod holders so they're parallel to the water. Then watch the tips closely as you drift. When the fish are aggressive, they'll pull the tip right down to the water; when they're not, you might just notice a light tapping that resembles a sunfish nibble. In most cases, it pays to set the hook at the first sign of a bite. Cats are voracious feeders and there is no reason to let them take the bait for more than a few seconds. With your rod now directly above the fish, your chances of a hookup are much improved.

Still-Fishing. Just because cats are holding in a certain depth range doesn't mean you can't catch them by still-fishing on the bottom. The trick is putting your bait where the thermocline intersects some kind of structure, such as a gradual shoreline break, a creek- or river-channel break, a point or a mid-lake hump.

If you have a boat rigged with a depth finder, putting your bait in the right zone shouldn't be a problem. You may even want to use your boat to look for the right depth zone and then pull it up on shore and toss out your bait.

If you're a shore-fisherman and don't know where to cast to put your bait at the right depth, try this: Toss out a slip-float rig and keep adjusting your bobber stop until the float lies on its side. Then reel in and measure the distance between the sinker and the stop—that's the depth of the water. Now you know exactly where to cast to keep your bait at the proper depth.

Despite all that's been written about catfish suspending during the summer, lots of catfishermen still labor under the assumption that cats go deep in hot weather. These anglers stubbornly continue to ply depths that haven't seen a catfish (or any other kind of fish) for weeks. They assume that the fish just aren't biting because of the hot weather.

If all this sounds familiar, it's time to change tactics and turn those dog days into cat days.

Tips for Catching Dog-Days Cats

Use a longer-than-normal rod (at least 7 feet) when slip-float fishing for suspended cats. With a long rod, it's easier to take up the slack that develops because of the right angle between your rod, the float and fish so you can get a firm hookset.

LAST-DITCH CATS

by Richard Alden Bean

With the explosion of interest in catfishing, it's becoming harder and harder to find a productive catfishing hole that hasn't been discovered by the masses. But that's not a problem if you happen to live in southern California. There, you'll find some unlikely hot spots—endless miles of irrigation canals and ditches that hold impressive numbers of catfish.

You might get the idea that these small waters produce only small cats, but that's far from the truth. "They catch some nice catfish out of the canals around here," said Roger McKenzie, who owns and operates Brewer's Bait and Tackle in the small farming community of Palo Verde. Channel cats, the most common of the three catfish species in the canals, weigh anywhere from a couple of pounds to as much as 15 pounds. Blue cats, though not as common, grow larger than the channels. Anglers regularly catch 10- to 20-pounders and have taken blues up to 50 pounds.

Flatheads offer by far the best chance for a real trophy. They're more common than blue cats and may reach a weight of 30 pounds or more. While fishing just below the return canal in the Palo Verde Lagoon in 1992, Virgil Grimes set the California flathead record with a 60-pound monster taken on a live bluegill.

Despite the quality of the fishery, the canals are lightly fished. "There are some local guys who just fish the canals even though the Palo Verde Lagoon and the river itself is nearby. You'll see them sitting in a lounge chair alongside the canals, just kicked back with their rods in holders waiting for the catfish to bite," McKenzie said, laughing.

The canals McKenzie refers to lie in the Palo Verde and Imperial valleys. This vast area used to be desert, but irrigation water from the Colorado River converted it into croplands.

The two valleys combined contain several thousand miles of canals designed to bring water from the Colorado River to the farm fields and then return it to the river. Practically all of this water holds catfish and is accessible to the public.

Besides catfish, these mini-rivers are filled with a wide assortment of fish that migrate in from the Colorado River including largemouth bass, smallmouth bass, striped bass, bluegill and even tilapia.

THE CANAL SYSTEM

To fish these waters properly, you must understand how the canal system works. Here's an example:

In Palo Verde Valley, the Palo Verde Irrigation District diverts water from the Colorado River several miles above Blythe, dumping it into large delivery canals that run down through the valley. Water is then taken from the largest canals and pumped into smaller delivery canals that take the water to the fields. A series of even smaller collection canals, or drainage ditches, gather up the "used" water and finally terminate in one large drain before returning to the main river.

The majority of the canals are simply excavations in the ground, but some are lined with concrete. The canals vary in size from 120 feet wide and 10 feet deep to only 20 feet wide and 4 feet deep (a few are even smaller). The Palo Verde Valley has several hundred miles of canals and irrigation ditches; the Imperial Valley, which runs from the Salton Sea to the Mexico border, more than 3,000 miles.

The larger canals generally have well-maintained dirt roads running on both sides. Unless they are marked with "No Trespassing" signs (which are not common), you pretty much have the run of the canals. You can drive along a canal until you find a likely spot, park your vehicle alongside the road and go fishing at your leisure.

At frequent points on the big canals, you'll find diversion gates, big pump houses and flow-regulating dams. Most of this is solid concrete structure, and any flow break or other change in depth or the structure of the side of the canal usually holds more cats than a featureless stretch of canal.

"Fishing in these water district canals is like structure

Ordinary guys with some extraordinary cats from the canals and ditches.

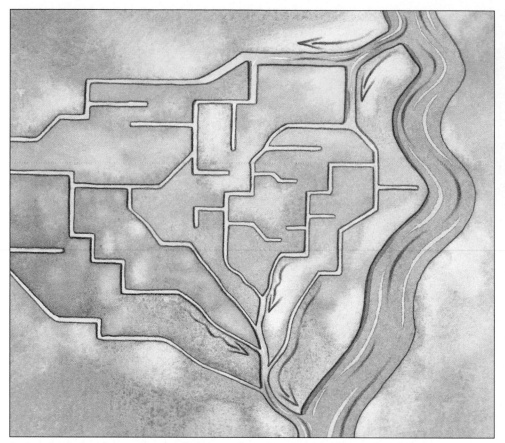

Irrigation canal systems are large and intricate. You'll need to be mobile to cover a lot of water and find fish. There are lots of places for them to be.

fishing in a lake," notes Jerry Murphy, a canal-fishing regular. Murphy looks for any kind of structural break in a canal such as a hole, indentation or bend.

Sometimes the structure is not easy to see. Murphy is constantly on the lookout for any deep holes scoured out by water rushing over control gates. Weed or moss beds are scarce because of winter drawdowns and dragging of the canal bottoms, but where you find them you'll also find catfish, he says.

Perhaps the very best spot, particularly for big cats, is underneath a road—any road. That shouldn't come as a surprise because catfish are known for their nocturnal habits, and the roadways offer a dimly lit refuge, even on the brightest day.

On larger canals, you'll find the fish beneath bridges. Smaller canals, however, may not have bridges; instead, the water passes under the road through a culvert.

But don't get the idea that these culverts won't attract catfish. They provide the dark hiding spots that cats love and few fishermen have discovered. In fact, a culvert makes a perfect ambush station for a hungry cat, because it funnels baitfish and other food items right to the fish.

FISHING THE CANALS

If you like "Huck Finn" style angling, you'll love fishing the irrigation canals. But sitting back in your lawn

chair and waiting for the fish to come to you is not necessarily the best method.

One good way to fish the larger canals is to partner with a fishing buddy. That way, you can fish all the likely looking spots along miles of canal by leapfrogging. One angler works a stretch of water while the other drives the vehicle a mile or so down the canal and works the next section. When the first angler gets to the vehicle, he then leapfrogs the second to work yet another section. Before long, you've covered several miles of the canal.

You can catch catfish in the canals any time of the year, but you must plan your fishing around the drawdowns.

"It's very good from April through December, until it starts to get real cold," says Jerry Murphy. "They drain most of the canals in January for maintenance, but some of the canals have deep holes and fish survive through the drawdown. Basically, the hotter it gets, the better the fishing."

Although most anglers plunk themselves down alongside a likely looking hole, toss out a slip-sinker rig, prop their rod up on a forked stick and then sit back and wait for a bite, others take a more active approach. Using a lighter slip-sinker rig or a slip-float setup, they let their bait drift along the bottom to cover more water and find the fish.

The drifting method also works well for fishing beneath a bridge or in a culvert. Just

Where to Find Catfish in the Canal System

Washout Holes. *During periods of heavy flow, water rushing over dams, diversion gates and other man-made structures excavates deep holes that are ideal for catfish.*

Outside Bends. *Just as current cuts into the outside bend of a river and creates a deep hole, current tends to excavate a hole wherever a canal makes a turn.*

Bridges. *Where a highway passes over a canal, the bridge provides a shady area where cats often congregate, assuming the water is deep enough and there is adequate cover.*

Ditches. *Don't overlook the big-catfish potential of the smaller ditches. The deeper ditches with a decent water flow will hold some good cats. If there is vegetative cover on the banks to shade the water and provide hiding spots, all the better.*

move to the upstream side of the road and let the bait drift slowly downstream. You'll catch plenty of channel cats, but it's not unusual to pull a big flathead or blue from a small culvert that would seem much too small for a fish of that size.

For channel cats, Murphy's favorite bait is fresh chicken livers. But he also uses nightcrawlers, cut bait (especially frozen mackerel and anchovy), cheesebait and bloodbait. Shrimp and clam meat will also catch channels.

Live baitfish are the best choice for flatheads, although some anglers prefer crayfish (beak hooked) and waterdogs (lip hooked). Murphy prefers bluegills and goldfish but notes that the latter may be

hard to find at bait shops. Other effective baitfish include small carp, redhorse and tilapia, which are easy to dipnet in the canals. Live baitfish will catch plenty of blues as well, but blues will also take any of the baits used for channels.

Tackle Selection

"I like lighter tackle myself," says Murphy. "With a light slip-sinker rig and chicken liver as bait (for channel cats), I like to bounce and roll the bait down the bottom in the current."

Murphy normally uses a medium-heavy-power spinning outfit with 10- to 12-pound mono for channel cats. Slip-sinkers could run any-

where from a half ounce for slow current to a couple of ounces if you're trying to anchor a bait in the turbulent, roaring tumult of water crashing over a flow gate.

You might think that it's safe to use very light tackle in the smaller, sluggish drainage ditches, but that's not the case because the smaller ditches often produce the larger cats.

While you can get by with relatively light tackle for most canal fishing, you'll obviously have to use beefier gear where there's a good chance of tangling with a big flathead or blue. These bruisers require a heavy baitcasting or medium-power saltwater spinning outfit with 20- to 30-pound mono or 30- to 50-pound superline. If you've ever tried horsing a

There are some big cats in these canals and ditches. Don't go too light on your tackle choices.

big catfish upstream to get it out of a culvert, you know why powerful tackle is a must.

The southern California canal system may well be America's best-kept catfishing secret. Every day, millions of people drive over the canals, never realizing that these murky waters are home to astounding numbers of catfish. Jerry Murphy and the other canal-fishing regulars hope it stays that way.

How to Hook Popular Canal Catfish Baits

Chicken Liver. *Wrap chicken liver in a piece of cheesecloth or nylon mesh to keep it from falling off the hook. Insert the hook through the bag so the point is exposed (top). You can also rig the bait on a safety-pin-style "liver hook" (bottom).*

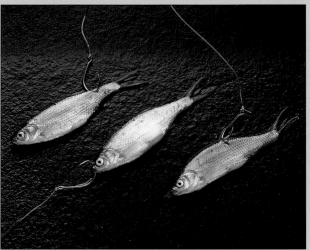

Live Baitfish. *When the current is light, hook a goldfish, shiner or other live baitfish through the tail (top). In faster current, they'll stay alive longer when hooked through the lips (middle). For float fishing, hook the bait under the dorsal fin (bottom).*

Dead Mackerel. *For channel cats, put a small piece of cut mackerel on a single hook (top). For big blues, cut a mackerel in half and push a size 6/0 to 8/0 saltwater hook through the lips (middle) or tail (bottom). Be sure to trim the tail first.*

Crayfish. *Hook a crayfish by pushing the hook through the bony "horn" on its head. Hooked this way, a crayfish is not likely to scoot backward, crawl under a rock and get you snagged.*

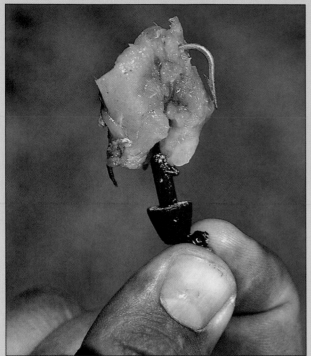

Search for catfish using a jig tipped with a piece of cut bait. Just cast out the jig, let it rest on the bottom for a few seconds, then move it a few feet and let it rest again. When you find some fish, switch to a slip-sinker or slip-float setup.

When fishing for flatheads and blues, dipnet baitfish such as bluegills, carp, redhorse and tilapia in weedy areas of the canal and in eddies that form along the edges of concrete walls and below diversion gates.

Use a long-handled landing net to reach catfish along steep-sided areas of the canal. With an ordinary net, you would have to climb down to the water's edge, possibly losing your footing or otherwise putting yourself in a precarious position.

Southern California's Membership Lakes

Southern California's canal system appeals to catfishermen who want to escape the crowds found on most of the region's public fishing waters. But anglers who prefer a more picturesque setting have discovered another option: membership lakes.

Typical of these waters is Oso Lake, a 220-acre impoundment nestled in the foothills of the Santa Ana Mountains, below Saddleback Peak. The lake, which is managed through a cooperative agreement between the Oso Sportsman Organization and the Santa Margarita Water District, is one of Southern California's best largemouth bass waters, but it also holds a thriving population of channel catfish along with a growing number of blues.

Anglers who purchase a family membership have access to clubhouse facilities, a boat dock, boat storage and rental boats rigged with electric motors. On weekends, members of the Oso Lake Sportsman Organization conduct on-the-water fishing classes for kids, with tackle donated by the fishing industry.

The general public can also sample the excellent catfishing at Oso Lake by simply calling ahead and booking reservations for a day of fishing.

There are two reasons why Oso Lake is such a good catfishing lake. First, the lake is managed as a catch-and-release fishing lake for all species. Second, only artificial baits rigged with barbless hooks are permitted as part of an extensive management program headed up by general manager, Bob Heerdt.

"We strongly support catch-and-release fishing. It is not only important in protecting our year-round fishing lake, but this unique conservation program ties right in with our youth education classes. Each season our trained staff of volunteers takes hundreds of kids fishing for catfish.

Oso Lake.

This first-time fishing experience is what we hope will provide these youngsters with an opportunity to make fishing a part of their adult life. The focus of the membership is to provide a good day of fishing on a nearby lake for everyone without hurting the catfish population," states Heerdt.

Only commercially prepared artificial baits are allowed when fishing for Oso Lake catfish. To protect water quality in the reservoir, no cut mackerel, anchovies, nightcrawlers, chicken liver or other traditional natural catfish baits are permitted.

The catch-and-release fishing regulation has proved very successful for both channel catfish and trophy largemouth bass. In fact, the lake-record largemouth stands at 16 pounds and there are plenty of bass in the 5- to 12-pound class. "We try to encourage all anglers to appreciate the potential of this fishery and respect the fish that they catch," says Heerdt. "The barbless hook makes it easy for a quick release of the hooked fish, no nets are allowed and anglers are instructed by our trained staff on the proper procedure for releasing a fish without taking it out of the water. All members police the

lake daily and will make it a point to spend some time with a new angler covering the techniques of gently releasing a fish and keeping it out of the water as little as possible. Lake policy does not encourage the use of rags to hold a fish prior to release in order to preserve the protective slime on the body of every fish caught in Oso Lake."

The Oso Lake record for channel catfish stands at $46\frac{1}{2}$ pounds, and divers checking out the dam and aeration system report seeing even bigger catfish following schools of suspended shad. Catfish caught by anglers generally run from 5 to 8 pounds. Due primarily to the warm water that is recycled through the lake, Oso's channel catfish feed all year long. Cold weather and a few winter storms may shut down the bite for a couple of days, but then the action picks up again.

Oso Lake Fees & Requirements
Family Membership - $500/yr.
Public Fee - $40/day.
Each member is required to take 10 disadvantaged kids fishing each year as part of the youth conservation program.

MEGA-CATS ON MINI-BAITS

by Clark Montgomery

You can't accuse Glen Stubblefield of being set in his ways. Like most other Kentucky Lake catmen, the veteran guide has found that the giant blues inhabiting the big lake are tough to catch in hot weather. But rather than targeting other kinds of fish during the heat of summer, like most of his competitors, Stubblefield was determined to find a way to catch the big blues when the water temperature started edging into the 80s.

Stubblefield soon discovered that the big fish were in deeper water than he and most other veteran anglers were fishing. "You could catch plenty of small catfish shallow, but the biggest ones seemed to prefer deeper water, especially the flats and dropoffs along the old Tennessee River channel," he says. "While other catmen were fishing 15-foot water, I found big fish between 25 and 45 feet deep. But what was most surprising to me was the fact that these deep fish fed actively all summer long. The catfishermen I knew who stayed in shallow water always hung up their rods in midsummer, but I found the hotter it got, the better the big cats would bite."

Stubblefield also discovered that location, by itself, did not guarantee blue-cat results. The big chunks of cut bait that worked so well during coolwater periods just weren't doing the job, so he began to experiment with a variety of live, dead and prepared baits.

Glen Stubblefield hoists a mega-blue.

Although the cats he was targeting had a mouth big enough to swallow a poodle, he soon learned that a big bait wasn't necessarily the ticket during the stifling-hot midsummer months.

"The hotter it got, the smaller the bait the big cats seemed to want," he notes. "I worked my way down in size from cut chunks of shad to nightcrawlers to crappie minnows, trying to see what turned 'em on the best."

Strange as it seems, Stubblefield determined that crappie minnows outfished every other bait. Nightcrawlers worked well too, but he got tired of white bass and panfish constantly cleaning them off his hook before they got to the bottom.

When Stubblefield refers to crappie minnows, he means fatheads, or "tuffies" as they're called throughout much of the South. He prefers minnows about 2 inches long.

"On one of the first trips where I tried crappie minnows, I caught a 35-pound blue cat. I thought this had to be a fluke, but I soon caught several more big cats on tuffies, so I kept playing with 'em."

But then he made an even more surprising discovery: In midsummer, dead crappie minnows outfished live ones 10 to 1 for cats exceeding 20 pounds! And the biggest cats really seem to crave them. Stubblefield has boated several blues exceeding 60 pounds on dead crappie minnows.

WHERE TO FIND GIANT BLUES

Knowing what areas hold the biggest catfish is essential to Glen Stubblefield's success. Years on the water have taught him that certain key structures will consistently attract big blues.

"I target what I call 'benches'—the old river banks just off the main channel that were high and dry before the dam was built and the lake formed," he notes. "On most reservoirs, the timber along the banks was cut down to stump level before the lake was filled. On lakes with a good current flow, trees float downstream and come to rest on these benches during floods. All of this wood attracts big cats if it's in the right depth zone."

Stubblefield has caught most of his monster cats in midsummer probing "benches" in the 25- to 35-foot zone.

Staying on his favorite spots is second nature to the seasoned guide; until you're totally familiar with the water you're fishing, he highly recommends dropping a series of widely spaced marker buoys to delineate the structure. If you do occasionally wander outside the lines and end up over the old river channel, don't worry. Stubblefield says big summer cats will often suspend in the channel at the depth of the closest "bench," and are highly catchable.

"The narrowest benches are often the best because they tend to concentrate a lot of fish," Stubblefield says. "Watch your graph as you move along with your rig bumping bottom; if you start edging into the channel more and more, the bench is probably narrowing. If there's a big sunken tree or a bunch of stumps on the narrow part of the bench, you could be in hawg heaven."

The more woody cover the better, Stubblefield insists. "One spot I fish forms a V-shaped point before dropping off on both sides into the river channel. Right at the tip of the V, there's a tremendous tangle of crisscrossing trees that have drifted into this hole over years of flooding. I've caught several blue cats over 50 pounds from this spot and have had other fish on that I simply couldn't handle. I've also left a ton of sinkers hung in the trees, but that's just part of the game. You ain't gonna catch cats unless you're knockin' that sinker around wood."

Another key spot is the juncture of two primary structures. "Offshore structure fishing is basically the same whether you're gunning for largemouth bass or catfish," Stubblefield explains. "If you're bumping your rig along the bottom off the main river channel and hit the area

Look for midsummer blues around rock piles, stump fields, brush piles, downed trees and other areas of dense cover along the old river channel. "Clean" structure holds considerably fewer fish.

where a creek channel intersects, you'd best be hangin' onto that rod tight. This is a key spot in the area for forage and predators alike."

Secondary structures such as ditches can make a sweet spot even sweeter, Stubblefield insists. "Look on the banks of your home lake and notice how little ditches, gullies and indentations drain water off the surrounding landscape. Now imagine these same ditches on a submerged river bank in 30 feet of water. Catfish use these as migration routes when moving from deep to shallow water. Watch for these slight indentations on the bottom with your graph; they aren't always evident on a topo map. Then just tap, tap, tap your way along them with that sinker until you connect with a cat."

Key Midsummer Catfish Locations

Narrow "benches" **(1)** *along the edge of the river channel concentrate midsummer blues. The narrower the bench, the easier it is to find the fish because they're bunched more tightly. Remember too that some cats will suspend over the channel* **(2)**, *usually at the same depth as the closest bench.*

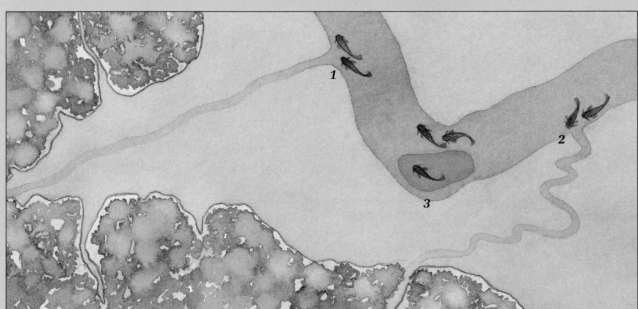

Catfish congregate around intersections of the river channel with **(1)** *creek channels and* **(2)** *small creeks and ditches. Another key catfish spot is* **(3)** *a sharp point along the river channel, where the fish have easy access to deep water.*

"Big bait, big fish" isn't always true, especially when summertime blues get the blues.

TECHNIQUES FOR GIANT BLUES

The thick cover that holds the big blues in midsummer is almost impossible to work with the usual methods, says Stubblefield. "Places with a lot of deep snags are tough to fish," he says. "You hang up constantly if you use the typical bottom-fishing techniques. So I started playing with some different presentations, trying to find the best way to probe thick cover without staying hung up."

After much experimentation, Stubblefield found that vertical presentation was the key to bagging big cats in deep, snaggy water. His approach is unorthodox but deadly.

He baits up with a dead crappie minnow by hooking it upward through both lips. If the bite is slow, he may spray a little garlic-scented Fish Formula on his dead tuffy.

The bait is fished on a 3-way rig (p. 105) with a double leader and a dropper that is lighter than the leader or main line. This way, even if one leg of the leader gets frayed, the other remains at full strength. And if the sinker snags, you won't lose the entire rig.

You'll need heavy tackle for horsing big cats out of the heavy cover. The ideal rig consists of a heavy-action 6½-foot baitcasting rod, a sturdy baitcasting reel with a low gear ratio (no more than 4.5:1) and 20- to 30-pound mono. A high-speed reel lacks the power needed to winch big cats out of the tangle.

Using a bow-mount trolling motor with the transducer of his graph attached to the skeg, Stubblefield works his way along the old river channel, with his line directly under the boat. Because his graph is mounted on the front deck, he can see exactly what's beneath the bow of the boat. This setup is essential to his catfishing system.

Sitting comfortably in the bow seat of his bass boat, he lowers the rig vertically, tapping the sinker on the bottom as he moves along the structure. "It's important not to drag the sinker along or it'll hang up on the first snag in its path," he warns. "Just raise and lower the rod gently so the sinker makes frequent, but not constant, bottom contact. As soon as you feel bottom, gently lift the rod—don't jerk like you would if you were fishing a jigging spoon for bass. Then lower it until you feel bottom again, and repeat. When you detect a bite, lower the rod, reel up some slack and set the hook hard."

Kentucky Lake is a river-run reservoir, so it's important to pay attention to the current, which fluctuates because of the generating schedule. Stubblefield has found that the bite is best when the water is moving a little—especially in midsummer. To keep his bait drifting slowly, he points the nose of his boat into the flow and trolls just fast enough so the boat "slips" slowly downstream (p. 105) while the sinker bumps bottom.

Right now you're probably thinking, "There are some things about Stubblefield's technique that make no sense." Why, for example, would a monster cat take such a tiny bait? You'd think the fish would burn up more energy catching a crappie minnow than it would gain by eating it. But the morsel is evidently just what a big cat wants when warm water puts it in a funk.

Another thing that's even harder to explain: Why would a veteran guide think of trying such a tiny bait for such a huge fish, and how did he manage to put the whole summertime blue-cat puzzle together—including the locational pattern and presentation method?

Simple. He's a catfish pro!

Rigging Up for Hot-Weather Blues

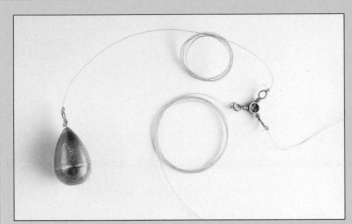

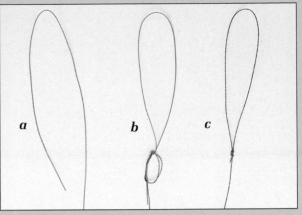

1 Tie a 3-way swivel to the end of your main line (20- to 30-pound mono), then attach an 18- to 24-inch dropper (12- to 15-pound mono) with a 1- to 2-ounce bell sinker at the end. To the remaining eye, tie a leader (the same strength as your main line) about twice the length of your dropper.

2 Make a loop in your leader and secure it using a triple surgeon's knot. To tie the knot, **(a)** form a loop in the doubled line, **(b)** pass the end through the loop 3 times and **(c)** snug up the knot by pulling on the loop and the standing line.

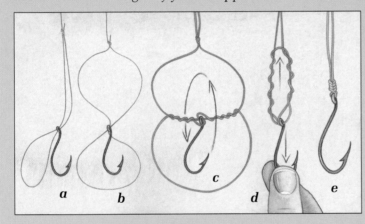

3 Attach the hook using a "cat's paw" knot by **(a)** threading the loop through the hook eye and **(b)** passing the hook through the end of the loop. **(c)** Continue to pass the hook through the loop and between the 2 leader strands until you complete 4 to 5 wraps, **(d)** snug up the knot by pulling on the opposite end of the leader while holding the hook, then **(e)** moisten the knot and pull it tight. The finished knot, which resembles a cat's paw, will not slip even if one strand of the leader breaks.

How to "Slip" the River Channel

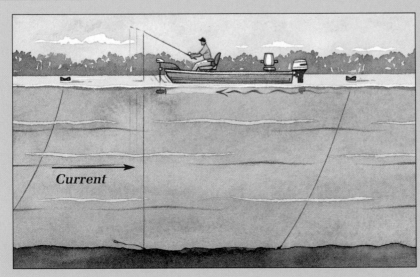

Drop a series of markers along the edge of the old river channel and then start fishing at the upstream end of the marked area. Point the bow of your boat into the current and run your trolling motor just fast enough to slow the speed at which the boat drifts downstream. Let your sinker touch bottom periodically but don't allow it to drag, and keep your line close to vertical. To fish the bench, follow the markers on the shallow side, but don't be afraid to try the deep side as well, because cats may suspend over the river channel.

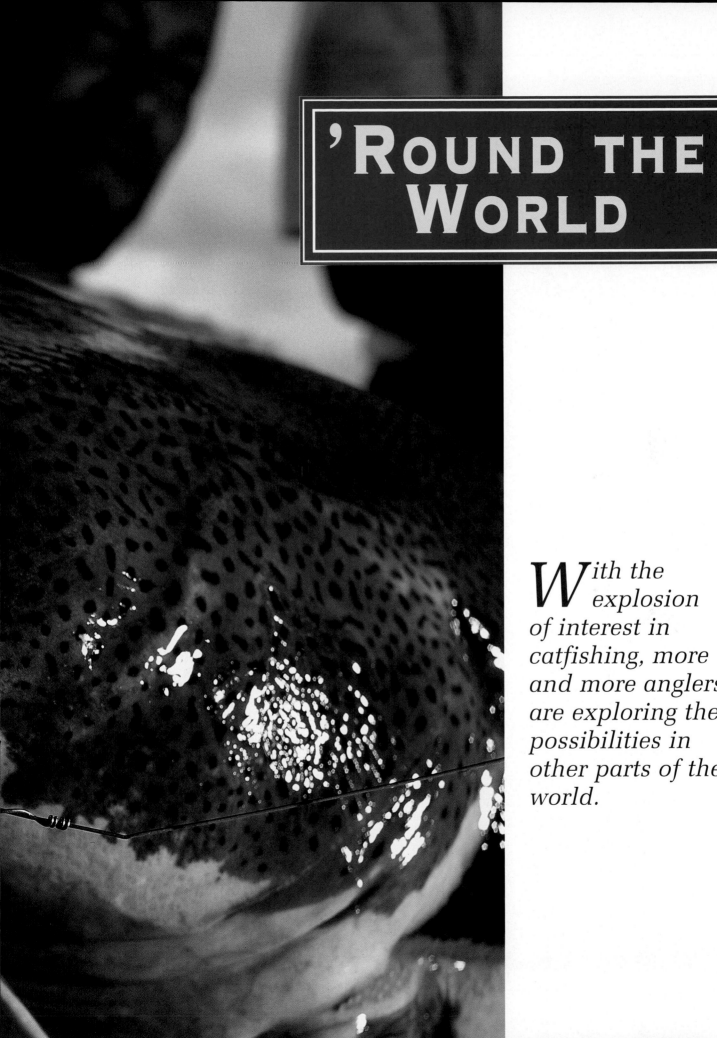

'ROUND THE WORLD

*W*ith the explosion of interest in catfishing, more and more anglers are exploring the possibilities in other parts of the world.

GIANT CATFISH OF THE AMAZON

by Paul Reiss, Garrett VeneKlasen and Dick Sternberg

No river system anywhere in the world is as rich in fish fauna as the Amazon basin. It is estimated that over 2,500 different species of fish occur in the Amazon. The order *Siluriformes*, or catfish, is the second most diverse and probably the most spectacular group of Amazon species. With 14 families, including about 1,000 species, Amazon catfish account for almost half of all the catfish species in the world.

Ranging in size from the tiny candiru (p. 113) to the gigantic Brachyplatystoma, or piraiba, these fishes occupy tremendously diverse ecological niches. Some are bottom dwellers, some nocturnal.

Some are parasites and some are roving predators. Some are completely scaleless while others are heavily covered with bony armor plates.

But the dense, remote Amazonian jungles have kept the biology and ecology of most of these species a secret—a secret that's not likely to be revealed anytime soon. In fact, it's likely that many Amazonian catfish species have yet to be discovered.

Here are some of the species you're likely to encounter on a trip to the Amazon.

Pirarara

The only South American catfish currently listed in the International Gamefish Association (IGFA) records are the pirarara, also called the redtail or red-tip catfish, and the dourada, or gilded catfish (p. 111).

Redtails are common throughout the Amazon and Orinoco basins, including blackwater and clearwater tributaries. They frequent deep holes, river confluences and wide pools formed at the junctures of rivers and lagoons. Redtails aggressively strike artificial lures including spoons, minnowbaits and rattlebaits.

The current record, 97 pounds, is held by the famous Brazilian angler and author, Gilberto Fernandes, but natives say these fish grow to around 120 pounds.

Pirarara (Phractocephalus hemiliopterus). *This is the only large Amazonian catfish with a bright orange tail and a huge, bony head.*

Piraiba

The piraiba is the biggest catfish in the Amazon (and the world), reaching a length of more than 9 feet. The taxonomy of this fish appears to be uncertain and the name "piraiba" probably includes two or more closely related species.

These fish are so huge that a separate name, "filhote" (meaning youngster or nestling), is given to the more commonly caught specimens (under 110 pounds). Piraiba are also known as pirahiba, lechero, zungaro saltón (Brazil) and valentón (Colombia).

Piraiba are widespread in the Amazon basin and can also be found in the Orinoco basin. They frequent the channels of large rivers, including muddy, blackwater and clearwater tributaries and the freshwater portions of estuaries. Large numbers of filhote can be found in flood-plain waters.

Gilberto Fernandes reports catching a 256-pounder on rod and reel, and one commercially caught specimen weighed in at an astounding 661 pounds.

Piraiba *(Brachyplatystoma filamentosum). The upper part of the body is dark or grayish and the belly is whitish. Smaller piraiba may be confused with piramutaba, but they have a much shorter adipose fin and there is no membrane connecting the 2 pairs of nares (nasal openings).*

Dourada

The dourada, also called dorado, dourada (Brazil) and plateado (Colombia), is the most common of the giant South American catfish. Because of its metallic coloration, it is sometimes called the gilded catfish. Dourada are found throughout both the Amazon and Orinoco basins.

Reaching a weight of up to 150 pounds and a length of more than 6 feet, the dourada has a habit of chasing schools of baitfish with its broad back and dorsal fin out of the water.

Found mainly in channels of large rivers, it often moves up on shallow floodplains to feed after dark.

Dourada (Brachyplatystoma flavicans). *Sporting beautiful metallic coloration with a platinum head and gold body, the adult dourada has relatively short barbels. Its tail is somewhat sharklike.*

It also inhabits muddy backwaters and clearwater tributaries, and frequently traverses rapids to reach tributary headwaters.

Surubim (Psuedoplatystoma fasciatum). *Surubim have vertical bars and a long, flattened head, accounting for the common name, tiger flathead. They are easily confused with caparari (p. 112), but the head and stripes are narrower.*

Surubim

This catfish is widespread in the Amazon basin and includes at least 14 closely related varieties with slightly different color patterns. At this time, the precise classification of the group is uncertain and it may turn out that there are several different species.

Surubim are also called tiger flathead, pintado, rayado, pintadillo (Colombia) and zúngaro doncella (Peru).

Found in all types of Amazon rivers, Surubim thrive in both running and still waters. They commonly swim upstream to headwaters areas and are seldom in estuaries.

Although surubim have been known to reach weights of 80 pounds, most weigh less than 30. Some varieties can be caught on the surface using flies and topwaters.

Caparari

In Brazil, these distinctly marked catfish are called caparari, but they're known as bagre tigre in Colombia and tigre zúngaro in Peru.

Like its close relative, the surubim (p. 111), the caparari is common throughout the Amazon basin, with the exception of estuary waters, and inhabits practically all types of running and still waters. But it seldom swims as far upstream as the Surubim and is rare in head-water areas.

Caparari are similar in size to surubim, commonly reaching a length of 4 feet.

Caparari (Pseudoplatystoma tigrinum). *The stripes are broader than those of the surubim and some of them are oblique or even horizontal, rather than all of them being nearly vertical.*

Piramutaba

The piramutaba is a close relative of the piraiba, but reaches only a small fraction of the size. Most piramutaba weigh in at less than 10 pounds, and individuals exceeding 30 pounds are quite rare.

Also known as mulher-ingrata and pirabotão in Brazil, the piramutaba goes by the name of pirabutón in Colombia and manitoa in Peru.

The piramutaba is found throughout most of the Amazon and Orinoco basins, mainly in channels of large muddy rivers. It is rare in blackwater and clearwater rivers. Piramutaba are more likely to inhabit the lower part of a river than the upper, and are sometimes found in the freshwater portion of estuaries. They seldom swim upstream past the first major rapids.

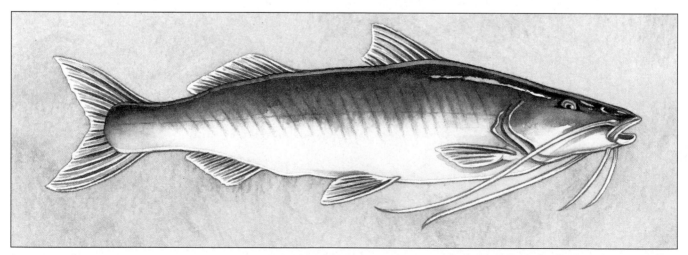

Piramutaba (Brachyplatystoma vaillantii). *The body is grayish above and whitish below, with a large adipose fin that distinguishes it from the piraiba.*

Secrets of the Catfish Pros

Jau

The jau is the most widely distributed of all the large Amazon catfish, inhabiting practically all types of South American rivers. Its range extends from Venezuela to northern Argentina.

It commonly swims upstream into headwater areas to spawn and can be found around steep rapids and waterfalls. Its blubbery body apparently protects it from being battered against rocks in the turbulent water. The jau has not been reported in estuaries.

Also called peje negro, chontaduro, pacamão (Brazil), pacamu (Colombia) and cunchi mama (Peru), the jau is the second-largest South American catfish. It is reputed to reach weights in excess of 250 pounds.

Jau (Paulicea lutkeni). *This is the only large South American catfish with a greenish gray body and short barbels. It has a blubbery body and bears some resemblance to the North American flathead catfish.*

The Dreaded Candiru

The candiru (*Vandellia cirrhosa*) is a tiny South American catfish that reaches a maximum length of only about 2 inches. Yet in some parts of Brazil, the candiru is dreaded by the natives.

This tiny parasitic catfish lives within the gill cavities of other freshwater fish, including large catfish species. Current produced by water moving through the gills of the host helps the candiru home in on its victim. Its slender form enables it to penetrate between the gills where its sharp teeth and spines on the gill cover start a flow of blood, which it sucks in with its mouth. The gill-cover spines also help the fish retain its hold on the host.

That may not sound too threatening to humans, but there can be a problem. When someone (male or female) bathing in a river urinates in the water, the candiru mistakes the flow for the respiratory current emitted by a fish. The candiru responds by darting into the swimmer's urethra, where it promptly extends its gill-cover spines to lock itself in place. If the invader is not promptly removed, it can work its way into the bladder and cause death from inflammation.

Years ago, a doctor traveling the Jurua district of the Amazon system reported examining 4 native males (a man and 3 boys) whose penises had been amputated as a result of a candiru intrusion.

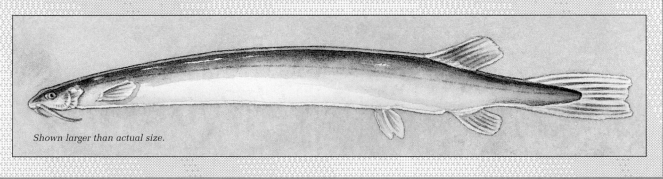

Shown larger than actual size.

WHERE TO FIND AMAZON CATFISH

Most of the large Amazon catfish are highly migratory, often moving 1,000 miles or more over the course of a year.

The entire region experiences a "dry season" and a "rainy season" which cause tremendous water fluctuations and have a great influence on catfish location. As a rule, the highest catfish concentrations occur during the start of and well into the rainy season.

Rivers north of the equator generally flood from April through November; those south of the equator, from December through May. As the flooding begins, huge numbers of baitfish are drawn upstream and the catfish are close behind. This migration is known as a "piracema." At the end of the rainy season, the baitfish move back downstream and the cats follow.

To be in the right place at the right time, it's important to know when the high-water period and piracema take place on the river you plan to fish.

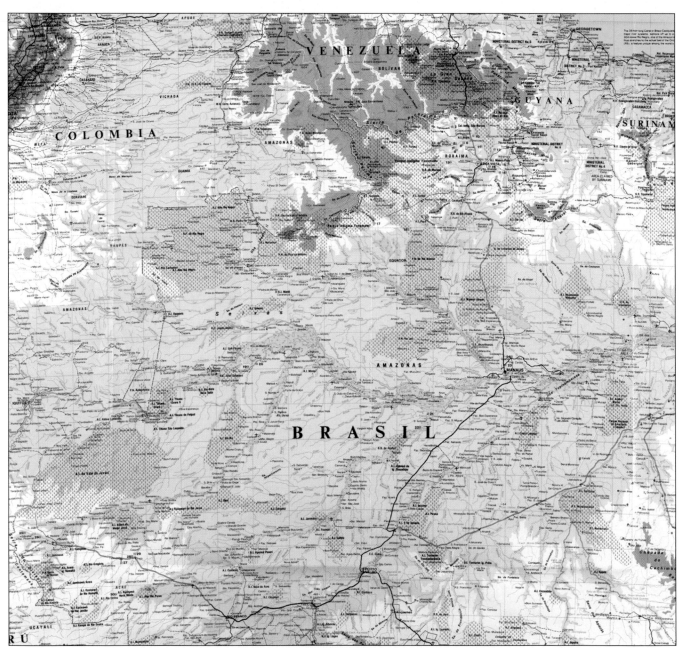

The Amazon basin—home to an exciting and virtually untapped catfishing mecca. Map provided courtesy of ITMB Publishing Ltd.

Some Amazon Catfish Waters

Large wing dams, usually found near major river towns, may offer the only rocky habitat in a stretch of river. Often, many kinds of catfish congregate in the washout hole below the wing dam.

The confluence of a tannic-stained "blackwater" river with a muddy "whitewater" river attracts large schools of baitfish that, in turn, draw a variety of catfish species. But if dolphins (porpoises) are present, you're not likely to find many catfish.

Deep slots (200 feet or more) in the main channel often hold large catfish species including piraiba, dorado and jau. You may be able to identify these slots by looking for large mats of floating vegetation.

Eddies along the shoreline, especially those with plenty of flooded vegetation, are ideal spots for small to medium-size catfish like surubim and pirarara. These eddies offer the shallower water and slower current that these species prefer.

Fishing for Amazon Cats

Many anglers who venture to the Amazon in search of its giant catfish come back with a lot of stories, but few catfish of the size they expected to see. It's not that the fish didn't cooperate—the anglers just couldn't land the giant cats they hooked.

The fighting habits of the big cats have been compared to those of large groupers. When hooked, they immediately head for the closest submerged tree or rock pile, and that's where they stay.

To have any chance of stopping the run and preventing a giant cat from reaching the snags, you'll need very sturdy tackle. In fact, many anglers use the type of "stand-up" gear popular among grouper fishermen and other saltwater anglers (right). At the very least, you should have a heavy-power catfish outfit with 50-pound-test line—something comparable to what you would use for the largest North American cats.

The baits, rigs and methods you use depend on the type of catfish you're most likely to catch. Redtails and surubim, for example, do not hesitate to strike artificials such as large spoons, minnowbaits and rattlebaits. And some varieties of surubim can readily be caught on flies as well

A good "stand-up" outfit consists of a powerful 5½- to 7-foot, long-handled boat rod and a large-capacity saltwater reel (no level wind) spooled with 200 yards of 60- to 80-pound mono. The reel must have brackets to which the clips of a shoulder brace can be attached, and the rod should have a gimbal butt that seats into the rod holder (inset) so the rod cannot twist when you're fighting the fish.

as poppers, chuggers, stickbaits and other topwaters.

But the vast majority of Amazon cats are taken on either live baitfish or cut bait, with piranha being the most popular type, mainly because it's the easiest to come by. Most anglers use a light bass outfit rigged with a small sinker and a size 2 hook with a small chunk of most any kind of "meat" for catching piranha and other baitfish. Small jigs also work well.

But piranha can be a downright nuisance when you're trying to fish cut bait for cat-

fish. If you use a mono leader, the scavenging predators will often slice it off in a heartbeat. The only solution is to use a heavy wire leader (below left). Piranha are much less likely to attack a fresh, lively baitfish.

Finding an Outfitter

A trip to the Amazon is obviously not something you want to attempt on your own. Your success—and maybe even your personal safety—depends on finding a reliable outfitter who has the equipment, guides and contacts necessary for such a complex undertaking.

If you like the comforts of a fishing lodge, you could head for Ecotur Lodge on the Branco River (800-336-9735) or the Xingu Lodge on the Xingu River (308-728-3884), both in Brazil.

If you're the more adventurous type, you might prefer a "mothership" operation in which you eat, sleep and

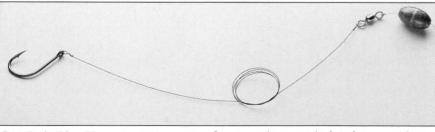

Cut-Bait Rig. *Haywire-twist a sturdy size 6/0 to 12/0 hook to a 3-foot, 60- to 90-pound-test, single-strand wire leader with a heavy barrel swivel haywired to the other end. Slide a 1- to 5-ounce egg sinker onto your line and attach the leader.*

travel on an 85-foot yacht and fish in 16-foot boats, along with a guide. You'll see a lot more country that way, and have a chance of catching giant cats that have never seen an angler's bait.

For more information on a mothership adventure, contact Paul Reiss at AcuteAngling, Califon, NJ, (908) 832-2987, or Garrett VeneKlasen at Interangler, Angel Fire, NM, (888) 347-4329.

Fishing from a mothership gives you access to water that sees little, if any, fishing pressure.

Hooked to a Freight Train *by Paul Reiss*

"Now that's a good-looking bait!" I thought to myself as I admired the piranha snapping its razor-sharp teeth as it hung from my hook.

To most anglers, the idea of using these bloodthirsty predators for bait may seem a little far-fetched but, when you're fishing for the giant catfish of the Amazon, they're nothing more than a morsel.

I tossed my baited rig out into the middle of the 5-acre pool, letting it sink the 20 feet or so to the bottom. I was starting to fidget around, looking for a comfortable spot in the boat when I felt the line in my hand start to slide away, definitely faster than the little piranha could pull it. I stripped line off my open bail, gave it 5 seconds, then closed the bail and cranked my rod tip down to the fish. Standing now, I leaned into the hookset and was rewarded with the feel of solid resistance.

Line immediately began peeling off my reel—not blazingly fast, but the fish moved steadily upstream, stopping about 50 yards from the boat. But when I started pumping the rod, the fish turned abruptly downstream, blowing right by the boat like a freight train. I now realized I was tangling with a big, strong fish.

I watched, at first in admiration, then in growing concern, as layers of line peeled off my spool. I quickly realized that drifting blithely behind this steamroller was only going to get me spooled, and fast. Before I could even shout, my guide had the motor running and the boat moving. The gold bottom of my spool was glinting through the windings of line before I began to gain some back.

The fish ran almost a quarter mile before taking a breather. We were long out of the pool and well downriver. I knew I couldn't let him rest, so once again I began lifting my rod and cranking it back down to regain line and keep pressure on the fish. But now space was at a premium. The river, swollen with recent rains, was normally about 75 yards wide here. Where the banks used to be, the water coursed hundreds of yards through the trees and into the jungle. And that's just where the cat was headed.

This time, the current was in my favor. Leading the brute steadily upriver, I was able to turn his head and keep him out of the jungle. I began to feel him tire now. Five minutes and several short runs later, my adversary sat below me, 20 feet under the boat.

Paul Reiss and a swimming freight train.

Now what? My light pack rod definitely wasn't built to haul huge fish off the bottom. Once again, the current came to my aid. As the boat drifted downstream, the angle improved and suddenly the giant came into view. My only reaction was, "Holy Cow!" I couldn't believe it! I had done it! A great surge of exultation coursed through me as my guide and I heaved the glistening red, yellow and black fish into the boat. He measured 52 inches from nose to tail, 37 inches in girth and an amazing 18 inches across his head. We estimated his weight at about 75 pounds.

Secrets of the Catfish Pros

WELS CATFISH: BIGGEST OF THE BIG

by Keith Lambert

Taxonomists recognize more than 2,000 species of catfish in the world today, the smallest of which reaches less than an inch in length; the largest, more than 15 feet. The latter, the European wels catfish (*Silurus glanis*), is possibly the world's largest freshwater fish.

Originally found only in Europe and Asia, wels catfish were introduced into the United Kingdom more than one hundred years ago by the Duke of Bedford who stocked them into his lakes at Woburn Abbey in Bedfordshire. Although the wels catfish is still considered a rarity in Britain, their distribution is increasing every year and there are now catfish waters in nearly every county in England.

Britain is almost at the most northerly point in the range of the wels catfish, so they are unlikely to ever attain the size of the huge fish captured on the continent, where the high temperatures and long summers coupled with large waterways and lakes ensure excellent growth rates.

Although there is no official world record for wels catfish, the biggest ever taken reportedly was over 16 feet long and weighed 675 pounds. In the U.K., wels cats grow to about 60 pounds and on rare occasion may reach 100.

BIOLOGY

Primarily scavengers, wels cats have a reputation for eating just about anything—live or dead. Captive wels cats have even been known to eat whole beef hearts. In the wild, some of their favorites include fish, mussels, crayfish, leeches, worms, and small birds and mammals. Large bony plates at the back of their mouth are used for cracking mussels and snails and crushing fish and other prey before swallowing them.

Wels cats detect their prey by both smell and vibration. Their barbels are equipped with very sensitive scent receptors, accounting for their acute sense of smell. They also possess a well developed "weberian apparatus," a chain of vertebral bones that helps amplify sound and vibration. Their tiny eyes reflect the fact that the fish

The wels catfish has a long muscular body with a small rounded tail that joins the anal fin and runs more than half the length of the body. The dorsal fin is tiny, even on a large fish. Wels cats have tiny eyes and a massive mouth that wraps around most of the head. Inside both lips are tiny teeth that feel like coarse sandpaper. At the top corners of the upper jaw are 2 long barbels; on the lower jaw, 4 shorter ones. Fish from clear water are usually very dark, often black or purplish; those from cloudy or discolored water, grayish or light brown. They generally have mottled flanks and cream- or white-colored undersides.

are primarily nocturnal and shun bright light.

The wels catfish has a tremendous growth rate, especially where there is an abundance of food. Water temperature also has a large bearing on growth rates, explaining why the fish grow so rapidly in countries that have long, hot summers such as those in central and southern Europe. In Spain for example, catfish were first stocked into the River Ebro system in 1978. Now there are plenty of 80- to 130-pound fish being caught, with the largest weighing about 165 pounds. Fish exceeding 200 pounds almost certainly swim in this river today.

Wels catfish spawn in spring and early summer, when the water temperature reaches a constant 68°F. The male builds a nest within the confines of tree roots such as willow or alder, but submerged vegetation is also used. After the female deposits her eggs in the nest, the male guards them until they hatch, which usually takes less than 5 days. He remains on guard until the fry are large enough to fend for themselves.

LOCATION

The wels prefers large waters with a soft bottom and slow current. During the day it hides much like a flathead does, coming out after dark to hunt for smaller fish.

After a hot spell, you'll often find the cats in the shallower areas of a lake, sometimes in only a foot of water. During colder weather, however, the fish will head for the deeper water.

You'll often find wels cats in the shaded areas beneath trees overhanging the bank.

They usually lie right where the roots and branches go into the water. You may be able to see the fish if you quietly creep into the bushes and peer into the water.

Another likely spot is a steep drop-off. The fish will often lie at the bottom of a shelf or in holes on the bottom. Surprisingly, muddy areas of the lake usually produce more cats than gravelly or sandy areas, probably because the soft bottom is rich in bloodworms and other invertebrates that the catfish feed on.

Dense weedbeds are a sure bet for wels cats. Sometimes the fish burrow right into the weeds where you can't reach them, but you can fish alongside the weeds to catch any fish patrolling the edge of the weed bank.

Like flatheads, wels cats often take cover in discarded items on the bottom including oil drums and car bodies.

Premier Wels Catfish Waters

For a good chance of catching wels cats of more than 100 pounds, look to the big waterways of mainland Europe. Many of the continent's prime cat waters have been stocked within the last 2 decades and are proving to be some of the best catfisheries in the world.

The best-known wels cat rivers in Europe include the rivers Saone, Seille, Doubs, Tarn, Loire and Petit Rhone in France.

Germany has many fine catfish waters including the Rhine, Donau, Neckar, Main and Naab.

Although cats are relatively new in Spain, some of the biggest fish in Western Europe reside in the Rio Ebro and its tributaries, the Segre and Cinca.

The mighty River Po drains much of northern Italy and has a thriving population of huge catfish that may approach 200 pounds. The smaller River Mincio also has a good population of wels catfish.

Few anglers venture into Eastern Europe, where commercial fishing is rife, but with a lot of research and perseverance, you can find good catfishing.

Large catfish exist in the Rivers Volga, Ural, Dnieper and Don in Russia, the Danube in Hungary and Romania, and the huge Vranov Reservoir system in The Czech Republic.

In Asia, Kazahkstan introduced catfish in the mid-1900s and the fish now reach huge proportions with monsters over 220 pounds caught every year.

HOW TO CATCH WELS CATS

Although many of the techniques used for catching wels cats are similar to those used for North American cats, others bear no similarity whatsoever. Here are some of the most popular tactics for taking wels cats in Europe and Britain.

Klonking

In recent years, "klonking" has emerged as the most effective method for catching wels catfish in European rivers. The technique gets its name from a wooden hand tool known as a *klonk* that makes an unusual and deeply resonant sound as the angler swishes it through water, attracting wels cats to the bait.

Here's how the method works: While drifting with a baitfish suspended below the boat, stroke the klonk back and forth. The faster the current, the faster the klonking (one stroke per second is usually adequate).

Use a depth finder to keep your boat in the deepest runs, which will generally hold the most and biggest fish. Make sure you have stout tackle and keep a firm grip on your rod, because a cat agitated by klonking may literally rip it right out of your hand! But not all strikes are that viscious; sometimes the fish only nip at the bait's tail.

Legering

The term "legering" simply means bottom-fishing, but ordinary bottom rigs don't work well on heavily fished waters, because the fish soon learn to recognize the resis-

---

---

tance of a bait tethered to a fixed sinker. But a "running leger rig" (the English version of a slip-sinker rig) allows you to fish a large live bait on the bottom, yet offers little resistance when a cat picks up the bait and swims off.

One problem with legered baits: They may lie motionless on the bottom, so they do not emit the strong vibrations needed to draw cats.

The solution is to use a polystyrene ball to float the bait off bottom so it keeps swimming. As a rule, it takes a ball about 1 inch in diameter to float a ½-pound baitfish.

How to Make a Running Leger Rig

Thread a 3- to 6-ounce bell-style sinker (called an Arlesey bomb) onto your line, add a barrel swivel for a stop and then tie on a 2- to 3-foot leader (25- to 40-pound mono) and a size 4/0 to 8/0 hook. If you want to float the bait off the bottom, thread a polystyrene ball onto your leader before adding the hook, and secure it with a pair of bobber stops.

With a pair of boat rods in rod holders and another pair of shorter rods fishing straight behind the boat, you can cover a swath of water up to 25 feet wide.

Float Fishing with "Boat Rods"

Float fishing from an anchored boat is one of the most exciting kinds of catfishing, especially at night. There's a certain magic to watching floats fitted with "starlights" (p. 123) bobbing around the boat.

To keep their floats spread well apart, some anglers use "boat rods," which measure more than 10 feet in length. The rods are placed in rod holders that hold them at right angles to the gunwales, so they fish almost like outriggers. This enables you to cover plenty of water with your live baits. The rods at the rear fish straight behind the boat, resulting in an even better spread.

Because of the wels cat's willingness to eat just about

any kind of food that will fit into its mouth, anglers have a nearly endless choice of baits. Here are some of the more popular choices:

Live Baitfish. Fish are one of the main items in the diet of a wels catfish, so most anglers start with a live baitfish. But some baitfish are better than others. Tench, carp and eels are good choices—they are hardy baits and can often be used for a long time before they tire. The predominant baitfish species in a body of water will generally make good bait as well.

Live baitfish are usually hooked through the top lip and out the nostril, although some anglers prefer to hook them through the base of the tail. Carry hooks (preferably offset models) in sizes 2 to 12/0 and select one that suits the size of your bait. Outsized

baits (2 to 3 pounds) may require a double-hook rig.

Dead Baitfish. Smelly dead baits, especially sea baits such as sprat, herring, whitebait and mackerel, are also effective for wels cats. Freshwater baits, particularly eel sections or baits that have been allowed to go bad, will catch fish as well.

Dead baits have several advantages: They work well for chumming and you can store them in your freezer so they're always available. Although they're generally used for bank fishing, cut bait is also a good choice for legering from a boat.

Other Baits. Although live or dead baitfish are the choice of most serious wels cat anglers, there are times when other kinds of baits work as well or better. Here are some of the options:

• Horse or medicine leeches. Unlike worms, these are almost a "wels-catfish-only bait," rarely being taken by other species. They work especially well for legering, but you must use a small float on your leader to prevent the leech from burrowing into the mud.

• Large mussels (with shells removed). Some anglers put two or more on the hook.

• Several worms gobbed onto a hook. Catfish love worms but, the problem is, so does practically every other fish.

• Small dead animals such as mice, voles, rats and birds are readily eaten by catfish

and make good baits on certain waters.

• Squid and cuttlefish are popular for klonking.

• If you chum your fishing spot with grocery baits such as sausages, liver or luncheon meat, you can use these same items for bait when you return to fish.

Tips for Catching Wels Cats

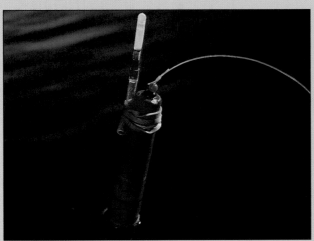

To make a "starlight" rig, attach a small Cyalume light stick to the top of your float using a rubber band. The light stick glows brightly and sticks up high enough that it is easy to see from a distance.

Push a small Cyalume light stick into a 1- to 2-inch polystyrene float attached to the hook of a leger rig with a piece of mono (length depends on water depth). This rig functions like a floating leger rig (p. 121) but works better for night fishing because the float is visible.

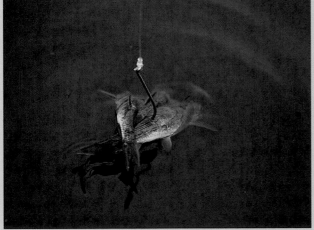

Keep your baits moving by using 2 or 3 smaller fish (such as tench or gudgeon) on your hook, rather than 1 large one. This way, the fish will continually "rattle" against each other instead of lying motionless on the bottom.

Keep a lively baitfish on the hook by pushing a ¼-inch piece of a wide rubber band over the hook point.

QUICK HITTERS

*I*f you study these short yet detailed accounts of methods used by the country's most successful catfishermen, you'll see a big improvement in your own catfishing results.

INTERSECTIONS ARE IT

You can't question the big-cat credentials of Darrell Van Vactor, a 21-year-veteran fishing guide from Calvert City, Kentucky, and the tournament director for America Outdoors (the Crappiethon people). Van Vactor has developed a remarkably productive technique for pulling giant cats, both blues and flatheads, from their deepwater lairs in Kentucky Lake.

In one recent 3-week period, he boated 16 blue catfish over 35 pounds, including giants of 74, 68, 54 and 46 pounds. And all of his fish were taken on light spinning tackle and 12-pound line!

Van Vactor catches most of his big cats from mid-August through mid-October. "Big catfish really are quite lazy," he explains. "Their cumbersome size virtually prohibits them from chasing baitfish, so they simply lay in wait for the bait to come to them. At that time of the year, these cats will hold in water that is 30 to 38 feet deep, and they will position themselves in a cut, ditch or channel that intersects the old river channel. I look for bends in the old river channel that are situated so that the current flows directly into them."

"When you find an area of this sort, the catfish will usually be situated at the downstream corner of that intersection so that the current sweeps food and baitfish right to them."

To catch these monstrous cats, Van Vactor positions his boat directly on top of the ditch or cut and lowers a live,

Darrell Van Vactor with a good flathead from an intersection.

4- to 5-inch river herring directly under the boat.

His terminal tackle rig consists of a 1-ounce egg sinker "toothpicked" onto the line a foot above a stout 4/0 hook. A live river herring, which he catches by casting tiny jigs into the turbine roils below Kentucky dam, is hooked just behind the dorsal fin.

"Big cats are not dumb creatures," Van Vactor says, "and I don't think you can catch them without using natural bait. I prefer live river herring, though they are extremely difficult to keep alive. I'll catch a dozen or so and keep them in a well-aerated live well, and when they are either gone or dead, I'll go catch more. Fresh, live bait is a key to this tactic, I believe."

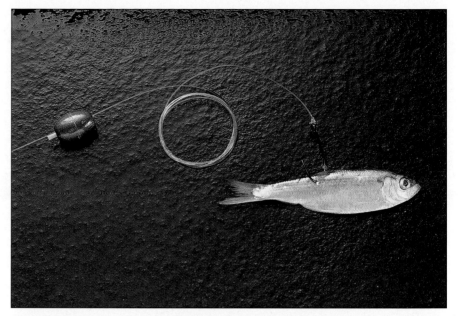

Thread a 1-ounce egg sinker onto the line, add a size 4/0 hook and secure the sinker by wedging it in place with a piece of toothpick. Then hook a river herring just behind the dorsal fin. With the sinker rigged this way, there are no knots to weaken the line, and the sinker can be easily moved to adjust the leader length.

Cats at the Intersection

Catfish congregate in areas where moving water in the old river channel (1) washes food into a ditch, cut, side channel or other kind of depression (2). The best spots are usually located on bends, because they create a natural flow into the depression. In most cases, catfish usually hold along the downstream edge of the depression, which is the most advantageous feeding spot.

THE SUMMER SKIPJACK BITE

Skipjack herring are common in nearly all big rivers inhabited by blue cats. They comprise a major portion of the blue cat's diet in some areas, and many catfishermen use them for bait. They're easily captured in cast nets or on small jigs.

Like shad, skipjacks are active baitfish, moving about continuously in large schools. But unlike shad, which feed primarily on microscopic plants and animals, skipjacks are piscivorous, favoring minnows, shad and other small fishes. This fact makes them doubly attractive to blue cats, especially in late summer. Here's why.

In July and August, large schools of skipjacks often churn the surface of the water as they pursue young-of-the-year shad (opposite). This is a highly visible phenomenon, quite similar to the surface-feeding melees of stripers and white bass. You can see the fish swirling near the surface, with little shad squirting all about as they try to elude the skipjacks. This activity usually occurs near dawn and dusk, frequently near creek mouths or at the junction of two big rivers.

When surfacing skipjacks are sighted, it's likely that scores of blue cats are lurking below, according to Keith Sutton, one of the country's best-known catfish writers and an accomplished catfish angler. The blues are attracted not only by the prospect of a skipjack entrée, but also by the many dead and crippled shad left behind when skipjacks slash through a school. Sometimes striped or white bass join the feeding frenzy, too, working on skipjacks and shad alike. This increases the number of injured baitfish fluttering about, another drawing card for gluttonous blues.

For the dyed-in-the-wool blue cat angler, this is an opportunity like no other. It's arguably the easiest chance you'll ever have to tag a monster blue.

Keith Sutton holds up a big blue from the summer skipjack bite.

In mid- to late summer, skipjack herring begin herding schools of small shad to the surface and, during the feeding frenzy, many of the shad are injured. As they float down, blue cats move in to begin the feast. The blues may feed on live skipjacks as well. Sometimes schools of white and striped bass join in the frenzy, injuring even more shad and drawing more blues.

Catching & Rigging Skipjack for Giant Blues

Catch skipjack several at a time by casting a Mustad Piscator rig, which has several fly-like lures and a weight on the end, into the roiling water below a dam or at the mouth of a tributary.

Cut a skipjack into 3 pieces—head, tail and middle. Hook the head piece through the eye sockets using a size 3/0 to 4/0 wide-bend hook; the middle and tail sections are hooked through one side and out the other so the hook pierces the skin twice. How much weight you need (if any) depends on the depth of the fish.

CATS BENEATH YOUR FEET

A long rod not only makes it easier to control your float, it helps you get a strong hookset when the rig is far from the boat.

Tim Scott, a part-time guide on the Illinois and several other rivers, spends 80 to 100 days a year chasing channel cats. But his approach might surprise some anglers. Instead of fishing deep holes and runs—the spots where most fishermen expect to find cats—he spends much of his time working shallow water only a few feet from the bank.

"This is a perfect opportunity for shore fishermen," says Scott. "Many times channel cats could be just 5 feet from where they're standing."

Scott always looks for riprap areas when he's targeting shallow channel cats. But his interpretation of riprap is somewhat generous. "I classify it in one of two categories," he explains, "man-made and

natural." Man-made riprap is what we're all familiar with— broken or chunk rock placed as an erosion barrier. Natural riprap, he says, could be anything from a rocky shoreline to jumbled timber along the bank. "It's got to have nooks and crannies where forage and catfish can hide, and it has to slow the current enough so channel cats will use the area."

This slower-water zone, which Scott calls "the catfish crease," extends about 5 or 10 feet from shore. He targets the crease from early May to July, when the water temperature is climbing from about 55 to 75°F.

Channel cats spawn at water temperatures in the 70 to 75°F range and, as spawning time approaches, his

target area moves farther up the riprap. "About the first week in July, I may catch all my fish in 1 to 3 feet of water," he says, "just 2 feet from shore."

He anchors his boat parallel to and about 15 feet from the crease, lobs a float rig baited with live or cut shad about 20 yards ahead of the boat and drifts it down the crease as far as he can. Because the channel cats in his waters generally run from 3 to 12 pounds, he can get by with fairly light gear. Scott relies primarily on a medium-heavy spinning outfit with 12- to 14- pound-test, abrasion-resistant mono.

"You need at least a 7-foot rod in order to control the float," he explains. "As it drifts closer to the boat, you have to lift the rod tip to keep as much line out of the water as possible. Otherwise you have problems with drag. As it passes the boat, you drop the tip and let out line to keep the float in the crease."

"In some situations, where the current is stronger, or I want to drift the float farther downstream from the boat, I'll use an even longer rod— sometimes up to 11 feet."

You may have noticed that the methods Tim Scott uses for shallow-water channel cats are very similar to those used by Stu McKay on the Red River of the North (p. 48), even though the rivers these anglers fish are hundreds of miles apart. This fact should give you confidence to try these methods on your home waters.

How to Fish the Crease

Anchor in the crease (pink zone) and cast your slip-float rig upstream of the boat *(1)*. As the float drifts downstream, keep your rod tip high and reel up slack to keep your line out of the water and minimize drag. Otherwise, the current will put a belly in your line and cause the rig to drift too fast. When the float reaches the boat *(2)*, feed line as the rig continues drifting downstream *(3)*.

Tim Scott runs an 18-foot tunnel-jon boat with a 115-hp jet engine to navigate shallow river stretches. With this rig, he can safely motor through water only a few inches deep.

Scott often baits up with a whole shad by cutting open the belly and pushing a hook into the body cavity and out the rib cage. It's important to leave the insides intact for maximum scent. "No guts, no glory," he says.

FLY ROD CATS

Ed Davis holds 8 fly-rod world records for catfish.

Ed Davis of Fayetteville, North Carolina, is arguably the Tar Heel State's best known catman. He holds both the state blue cat record (a 78-pound, 8-ouncer taken in 1991) and the state flathead record (a 69-pounder taken in 1994). Both of these behemoths were caught in the Cape Fear River using chunks of eel for bait.

But Davis is not one to rest on his laurels. He recently became interested in flyrodding for catfish and is waging a relentless assault on the fly-fishing record book. A glance at the fly-rod records compiled by the National Fresh Water Fishing Hall of Fame reveals that Davis holds seven of the nine line-class records for blue catfish (the other two are open) as well as the 10-pound line-class record for flatheads.

Very little has been written on fly fishing for cats, so Davis has had to develop his own methods. "This approach is truly in its infancy, and every trip is a learning experience," he says. "Of course, the biggest shock to most catmen is that catfish will, in fact, take a fly."

Davis has caught channels and flatheads on flies, but his specialty is blues. "They'll readily eat a fly when they're feeding on baitfish," he notes. "At times, channels are so easy to catch on a fly, they're an absolute nuisance." Flatheads? "Yeah, they'll take a fly, too, but they're hard to hook. My experience has been that they spit it out immediately."

Davis has found that fall is the ideal time for flyrodding. "In fall, big blues gorge themselves on schools of threadfin shad near the surface," he explains. "As the baitfish school moves downstream, blues position themselves facing upstream and when they intercept the bait, they roll on the surface, filling their faces with shad. It's an awesome sight, seeing a 50- to 75-pound blue cat rolling on top like Flipper."

"Just lay a streamer fly in the school of bait, work it a little and hang on."

Davis often lets the fly sink a bit, then moves it with a gentle jig/twitch presentation. It's not unusual to see a cat swim right up and eat the fly. When that happens, he hammers it and prepares himself for a long, drawn-out battle. "It will easily take 30 minutes to land a big blue on a fly rod. If you get impatient, you'll start popping off fish."

Davis's biggest fly-rod blue, caught in July, '97, weighed 42 pounds, but he's hooked much larger fish. "I've had blues on my fly rod that easily weighed 70 pounds, but didn't boat them. Yeah, I think it's entirely possible to land a 100-pound-plus blue on a fly rod. Heck, tarpon fly fishermen boat 180-pounders, don't they? If you play your cards right, you can whip a really big fish on a fly rod."

You don't need expensive fly-fishing gear to catch cats. Davis uses a 10-weight Shakespeare Ugly Stik fly rod coupled with a Martin 72 fly reel spooled with 50 yards of Dacron backing and a weight-forward, sink-tip fly line. He makes his own 9-foot tapered leaders (below). He normally uses a mono tippet, but when he's getting bothered by gar and dogfish, he switches to a braided-wire tippet (Steelon Sevenstrand). "The Steelon leaders are super abrasion-resistant and flexible enough for fly-rod application," he notes.

The North Carolinian has found catfish aren't all that finicky about fly patterns and presentations. "The Deceiver

Davis's Favorite Catfish Flies

Seaducer

Seaducer

Deceiver

Thiebault Needlefish

Bighorn Sardine

Deceiver

streamer pattern, popular with saltwater fishermen, is a good choice. Red and white works fine under most conditions; blue cats seem to like some tinsel tied in, too. In off-colored water, chartreuse and other bright colors sometimes produce better. I caught my 42-pound blue on a yellow perch pattern."

A stout hook is mandatory for catfish, Davis advises. "The hooks on most freshwater flies are way too small and light for catfish application. A quality cat will easily straighten a size 2 or 4 freshwater hook. Stick to saltwater flies, which have bigger, stouter hooks—streamers with size 1/0 to 3/0 hooks are highly recommended."

Unlike other kinds of fly fishing, there's not much finesse involved in fly fishing for cats, says Davis. "If you think of fly fishing as a 'gentle persuasion,' tying into a 40-pound blue on a fly rod will turn your head around."

Rigging Up: Leaders

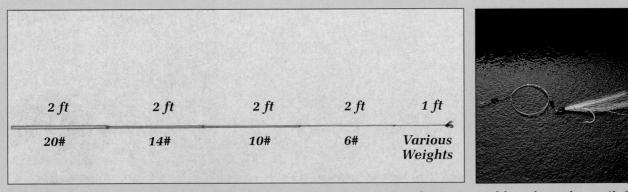

2 ft	2 ft	2 ft	2 ft	1 ft
20#	14#	10#	6#	Various Weights

Make a 9-foot tapered leader using 5 sections of mono varying in diameter and length as shown (left). Connect the sections using blood knots or double surgeon's knots. Davis varies the weight of his tippet depending on what line-class record he's pursuing. When using a braided-wire tippet, make loops in the ends using small crimps (right) for connecting the mono leader and fly.

TIPS FOR TROPHY FLATHEADS

Catching trophy flatheads doesn't happen every day, even for those anglers thoroughly familiar with their habits. As one avid flathead angler put it, "Fishin' for big flatheads is like trophy muskie fishing, only lonelier." You may spend hundreds of fishless hours trying to pinpoint a single trophy fish. And as the hours pass, the doubts begin to grow and you start wondering if it's really worth the bother.

That's why many anglers give up flathead fishing even before they land their first big fish: They just don't have the patience. But patience alone won't do the trick. Here are some tips from Jim Moyer, one of the country's best-known trophy hunters, that will help tip the odds in your favor:

• **Fish the warm months.** For the best chance of catching a trophy, do your fishing when the water temperature ranges between the low 70s and the mid-80s; that's when flatheads are most active. May through September is peak flathead fishing season in most parts of the country.

In the South, however, flatheads can be caught year-round, even during the coldest days of the year. Some of the largest flatheads on record were taken in February, March, October and December.

• **Focus on large rivers and lakes.** Trophy flatheads seldom come from creeks, ponds and small lakes. It happens occasionally, but not often enough to merit your attention. The true heavyweights almost always come from big waters.

• **Be a night owl, or at least an early bird.** Big flatheads are primarily nocturnal feeders; whenever possible, anglers should be on the water during

Trophy flatheads are freshwater fishing's biggest challenge—both size of fish and what it takes to catch one. This is Illinois River catfish guide Tim Scott.

hours of darkness. But if you have to work the next day, you probably don't want to stay up all night.

Here's another option: Try fishing the hours around daybreak, 4 A.M. to 8 A.M. On many waters, peak feeding activity occurs just as the sun is cracking the horizon. Sometimes the sunrise bite lasts an hour, sometimes two or three. But flatheads usually finish their feeding spree by 8.

•**Invest in good heavy tackle.** If you want to land that trophy when it finally grabs your bait, don't buy cheap, light-duty tackle. Otherwise, you might see your rod snapped in two like a stick of dry spaghetti, or your reel turned into a hunk of inoperable metal and graphite.

Most serious flatheaders favor saltwater surf-casting rods 8 to 12 feet long, big heavy-duty level-wind or spinning reels, and at least 30- to 50-pound-test line. Forty-pound line is about right in most waters, but if there are snags, you may have to go heavier—70- to 80-pound.

•**Use live fish for bait, nothing else.** The best bait is the type of forage fish that flatheads eat naturally in the body of water you're fishing.

Sunrise is prime flathead time.

Shad and sunfish are the primary foods in many waters, but chubs, small carp, bullheads and suckers also make up a large part of the diet in some rivers and lakes.

You'll rarely catch flatheads using chicken liver, stinkbaits and other dead, malodorous allurements that may tempt blue and channel catfish.

Heavy tackle is a must for big flatheads.

The best live bait for flatheads is what they normally eat.

Barry Mullin with a good Texas tidal marsh blue.

BLUES IN TIDAL MARSHES

Barry Mullin of Nederland, Texas, fishes for winter blue cats in the brackish waters of coastal southeast Texas. His favorite honeyhole is Bessie Heights Marsh near the mouth of the Neches River. The Neches flows into Sabine Lake, a bay that empties into the Gulf of Mexico.

"This area of the river is the threshold between salt and fresh water," says Mullin. "There is a huge salt marsh on the east side of the river and some on the west."

"When there's plenty of rain," he continues, "the runoff purges all the salt water out of the river and marsh. This sometimes happens in summer, and nearly always when the cold fronts

make their way down in winter. In December, the blue cats begin showing up. The years when it rains a lot in fall, more catfish move down the river than normal."

Mullin fishes in deep holes in canals feeding the marsh. These holes occur wherever the tide enters the canals from the shallows.

"When the weather is mild, and the shallow water temperature is warmer than the canals, blue cats often move into 2 feet of water or less in the open marsh," Mullin reports. "I look for places where the tide has cut trenches in the shallow marsh. A trench in shallow water is likely to hold blue cats, especially if it's near a hump cov-

ered with submerged grass. Blue cats are attracted to baitfish that are hiding in the grass and eating algae growing on the grass and mud."

"I use cut bait to give the fish a scent trail to follow, and usually catch baitfish that are abundant in the area I'm fishing—typically mullet, shad or croakers. Shrimp also are good bait. I often chum with the same type bait I'm using."

The pieces of bait Mullin uses are surprisingly small. He fishes them on a slip-sinker setup with a $1/2$- to 1-ounce bullet or egg sinker and a size 4 wide-bend hook. "I start with a bait the length of my thumbnail," he says. "If I'm catching too many little cats, I double the bait size. At times, the bigger blues want live bait only."

Blue cats position themselves to intercept baitfish being carried by the tide. Mullin says an incoming tide is best when fishing the shallow flats. When the tide is leaving the marsh, the catfish hold in holes created by swift current entering the canals. Catfish in Bessie Heights rarely bite when the tide is still.

"The most I've caught in one day has been 23 keeper-size blues, the biggest being 15 pounds. Four or five keeper-size fish is a normal day. I have caught several blues in the 12- to 15-pound range,

and know of one 32-pound blue caught in one of the canals."

We have a lot yet to learn about catfish in tidal waters, but the tactics outlined here can help you catch brackish-water cats now. Check with your state fisheries department to determine which tidal rivers harbor catfish, then put your newfound knowledge to work this season.

Mullin has found that tidal blues prefer small baits. He normally rigs a ½- to 1-inch chunk of cut bait on a size 4 wide-bend hook and fishes it on a slip-rig with a ³/₈- to 1-ounce egg sinker.

Blue Cat Locations in Tidal Marshes

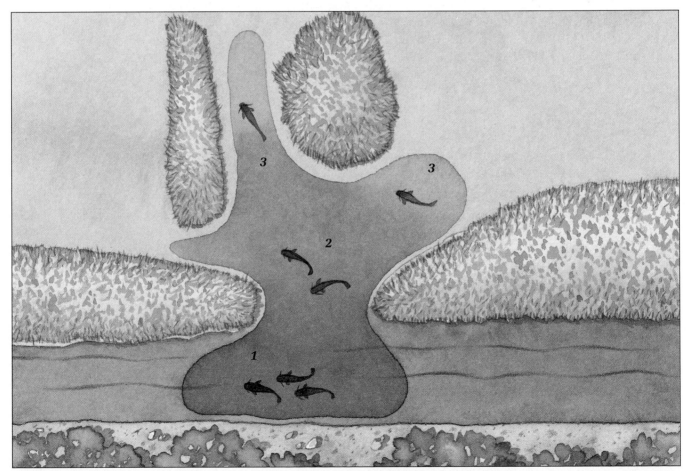

Look for blue cats in deep holes or trenches formed by tidal currents in (1) canals leading into tidal marshes and (2) the tidal marshes themselves. On sunny days in spring, you'll also find some cats on (3) shallow flats where the water is warmer than it is in the deep holes.

TIDEWATER WHITES

Roger Aziz Jr. of Methuen, Massachusetts, has fished for catfish in the tidewater rivers of his home state since boyhood.

Aziz ranks among the country's top white-cat anglers and has the credentials to prove it. He's caught several world line-class records from the Merrimack River, and the techniques he uses to catch big whites will work in other tidal rivers as well.

"The best fishing in the Merrimack is the tidal water between Haverhill and Newburyport, about 20 miles of river," Aziz reports. "The white cats here are current lovers. The only place you'll catch them is in the current. I wait for the tide to peak, and as the water starts to go back out, that's when I fish. You can catch whites when the current's coming up, but they're more spread out then. The best fishing is on an outgoing tide."

Aziz targets rocky stretches of river, the same areas frequented by striped bass and smallmouths. In upstream reaches of the 20-mile pool, he finds most whites in deeper holes. When fishing closer to the river's mouth, he targets white cats holding around bridge abutments.

He often fishes from shore using a 12-foot medium-heavy power spinning rod that allows a good long-distance hookset. When fishing from a boat, he prefers a 7-foot medium-power spinning rod. "Baitrunner" spinning reels spooled with 6- to 14-pound-test mono complete the outfits.

For bait, Aziz uses 1-inch chunks of cut shad or herring and often, bacon strips. "Bacon works best in spring," he says, "because there aren't any herring or shad moving in the river. I like to use a very sharp Kahle hook and get as much bacon on it as I can. A sharp hook will cut through the bacon and give you a good hookset. And I've

Roger Aziz Jr. hoists another nice Merrimack River tidewater white.

found that hickory-smoked bacon works best."

He normally fishes the bait on a no-roll sinker rig or a fish-finder rig (below). When the cats are holding in extremely deep water, however, he relies on small downriggers (below). But he uses the downriggers to still-fish while anchored, not to troll.

"Your line is connected to the ball, which is dropped to the bottom in deep holes with current," he explains. "Let out 6 to 7 feet of line away from the clamp (release) so your bait bounces in the current a foot or so above the bottom. When a fish grabs the bait, it trips the clamp, releasing your line, and you set the hook."

For Aziz and other cat fanatics in the Northeast, white cats are the essence of day-to-day fishing. "We get a few channel catfish and some bullheads, too," he says. "But there are more white catfish up here than any other catfish. They're the best thing going in this part of the world."

Rigging Up for Tidal Whites

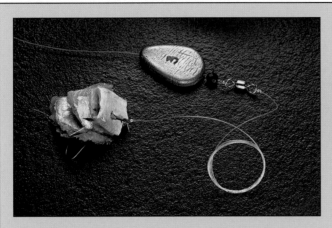

No-Roll Sinker Rig. *Thread a 2- to 3-ounce disc sinker onto your line, add a black bead and a barrel swivel and then tie on a size 3/0 wide-bend hook. The sinker will rest flat on the bottom and stay put, and the bait will ride a few inches above it.*

Fish-Finder Rig. *Thread a 2- to 3-ounce egg sinker onto the line, then add a barrel swivel and an 18-inch leader of 14-pound mono. Thread a Styrofoam ball onto the leader, add a bobber stop and tie on a size 3/0 wide-bend hook. Set the bobber stop to keep the ball in the middle of the leader; it will float your bait up high enough for cats to see it.*

Downrigger Fishing. *Clamp a small downrigger onto the transom or gunwale of your boat and attach a 6-pound ball with a release to the cable. Tie a wide-bend hook to your line, bait up, let out about 6 feet of line, attach it to the release and lower the ball to the desired depth while feeding line off your reel. Then place your rod in a holder and take up enough slack to put a bend in the rod. When a fish grabs the bait, it will pull the line out of the release and the rod will stand up straight.*

GREAT EATING

*O*nce you try
these recipes,
you'll understand
why catfish are
the hands-down
favorite of so
many fish
connoisseurs.

Greek-Fried Catfish (page 145)

CATFISH PREPARATION

by John Phillips

"Don't want no bream or crappie. Only one fish that makes me happy: Catfish, catfish."

– From the musical "Pumpboys & Dinettes"

The tremendous popularity of catfish as a food fish is easy to understand. Some would argue that cats are the tastiest of all gamefish but, beyond that, they're nutritious and have a low fat content. Compared to pork, various cuts of beef, and chicken, catfish is lowest in fat and second only to ground beef in protein content.

The huge demand for catfish has led to a multi-billion-dollar catfish-farming industry that supplies thousands of catfish-specialty restaurants around the country. But if you're a fisherman, you don't have to buy your cats—you'll have a lifetime supply.

There are thousands of tried-and-true catfish recipes, some of the best of which are shown on the pages to come. But before getting into specific recipes, you should know some of the basic rules of catfish preparation. Here are some tips for each of the major cooking methods.

Baking

Too much heat will cause catfish to become dry, shrink and fall apart. To avoid overcooking, follow the basic "10-Minute Rule" for whole or dressed fish, fillets, steaks and fingers.

First, measure the fish at its thickest part. If fresh or thawed, bake 10 to 12 minutes per inch of thickness. If frozen, bake 20 to 24 minutes per inch of thickness. If covered or cooking in a sauce, add an additional 5 minutes baking time per inch of thickness.

Bake at 450°F, testing for doneness after 2/3 of the cooking time has elapsed. Fish is done when the flesh becomes opaque and flakes easily when tested with a fork or skewer.

Microwaving

This method cuts cooking time by about 75 percent. Rather than the 10-Minute Rule, use the 3-Minute Rule per pound of fresh or thawed catfish (triple time for frozen) with a "high" setting. Always test for doneness after 2/3 of the time has elapsed. Rotate frequently.

To convert a recipe from conventional to microwave, decrease the liquid by 1/4 of the conventional recipe (1 cup stock - 1/4 cup = 3/4 cup stock), and decrease the cooking time by 3/4 of conventional (20 minutes at 450°F - 15 minutes = 5 minutes on "high").

Deep Frying

For best results, fill your pot half full of oil and heat to 375°F; any hotter and you may burn the fish.

Dip, dredge or batter, fry until golden brown and then drain on absorbent paper.

Avoid crowding and excessive handling when frying fish, and keep the temperature constant. If you're breading the fish, allow the coating to dry about 15 minutes before frying. Always discard dark, burned oil. Skim off any fried, crusty particles during frying, and strain the oil before storing for later use. Never add cool oil to heated oil; it will slow the cooking and spoil the taste.

Broiling

Place catfish on a preheated, lightly oiled broiler rack. Broil 4 inches from the heat source, according to the 10-Minute Rule, turning once during cooking. Baste frequently and test for doneness after 2/3 of the cooking time has elapsed to prevent the fish from drying out.

Grilling

A variation on oven-broiling, this method requires a well-oiled hot-grill rack and a little more distance from the hot coals. Cook with the 10-Minute Rule, basting frequently unless fish has been packaged in foil to prevent drying.

To build a cooking fire, start with a good bed of charcoal, 2 to 3 inches deep, so that it will last the entire cooking period. After starting the fire, wait for the coals to burn to a gray color with a ruddy glow underneath, which usually takes about 30 minutes.

CATFISH RECIPES

by Jim Casada and John Phillips

Armed with these recipes, you'll never again wonder how you're going to cook up your catch. You'll find some old standbys here, along with some ideas you've never seen before.

Part of the fun of catfishing is eating some of the fish you catch, now and again. Here's how to make the most of that bounty.

Blackened Cajun Catfish

1 T. paprika
2 1/2 tsp. salt
1 tsp. onion powder
1 tsp. garlic powder
1 tsp. cayenne pepper
3/4 tsp. white pepper
3/4 tsp. black pepper
1/2 tsp. thyme
1/2 tsp. oregano
6 catfish fillets
1/2 lb. unsalted butter
   melted (do not subsitute)

Preheat heavy skillet on outdoor grill at least 10 minutes until white ash forms in skillet bottom. Thoroughly combine paprika, salt, onion powder, garlic powder, cayenne pepper, white pepper, black pepper, thyme and oregano in small bowl. Dip fillets in melted butter so both sides are well coated. Sprinkle seasoning generously and evenly on both sides of fillets, patting in with hand. Place in hot skillet. Add 1 tablespoon butter over top of fillets. Cook 2 to 3 minutes on each side until charred. Serve with squeeze of lemon juice.

Catfish Amandine

4 (6- to 8-oz.) catfish fillets
Salt
Pepper
1/2 cup flour
1/3 cup oil
1/2 cup butter (do not substitute)
2/3 cup slivered almonds
1 lemon, thinly sliced
1 tsp. chopped parsley

Dry fillets thoroughly, salt and pepper each, and coat lightly with flour. Sauté in oil 5 to 7 minutes until golden brown, turning carefully, and then cook for the same time on other side. Remove catfish to heated platter.

Add butter to pan, and stir almonds to toast. (If desired, 1/2 cup cream may be added to toasted almonds in pan.) Heat just to boiling point before spooning over fish.

Spoon over fish, and garnish with lemon slices and parsley.

Baked Lemon Catfish

Catfish fillets
Lemon pepper

Spray pan with nonstick spray. Wash and drain fish. Sprinkle with lemon pepper on each side (or use garlic powder if preferred). Bake at 400°F in oven about 15 minutes on each side or until brown.

Catfish Parmigiana

1 1/2 lbs. catfish fillets,
   cut into serving pieces
1 (16-oz.) jar spaghetti sauce
2 T. chopped fresh parsley
1/2 T. basil
1 cup shredded mozzarella
   cheese
1/4 cup Parmesan cheese
Parsley sprigs

Grease 13 x 9-inch baking pan with margarine. Arrange fish in pan, and pour spaghetti sauce over fillets. Sprinkle parsley, basil and mozzarella cheese over fish. Bake in 350°F oven 20 to 25 minutes until fish flakes easily. Dust fillets with Parmesan cheese, and serve on heated platter. Garnish with parsley sprigs.

Tony's Catfish Swazela

6 large onions, sliced very thin
1 cup salad oil
1 (6-oz.) can tomato paste
3 large cans tomato sauce
2 green bell peppers, chopped
1/4 rib celery, chopped
1 cup cooking wine
1 (4-oz.) can mushrooms
2 T. Worcestershire sauce
1/2 cup green onion tops,
   chopped fine
1/2 lemon, sliced very thin
12 or 14 pieces of tenderloin
   catfish, 1/2 inch thick and
   about 6 inches in diameter
Creole seasoning

Sauté onions in salad oil until well cooked. Add tomato paste. Cook 5 minutes, stirring constantly. Add tomato sauce and cook 5 minutes.

A boy and his catfish catch, and dreams of the great eating to come.

creek banks while the fish were fresh. While the pot of catfish stew simmered over the pine fire, the fishermen continued catching cats).

> $^1/_2$ lb. bacon, diced
> 12 small onions, diced
> 6 lbs. catfish fillets
> 1 bottle ketchup
> 1 pod red pepper
> 1 clove garlic
> 1 lb. butter
> Salt
> Pepper
> 12 T. Worcestershire sauce

Fry bacon until crisp. Remove, and sauté onions in drippings until golden brown. Add small amount of water, and let onions steam until done.

In deep kettle, place layer of fish, then layer of onions, until all are used. Pour hot water over to barely cover fish and onions.

Add ketchup, red pepper, garlic, butter, salt, pepper and Worcestershire sauce. Let boil 20 minutes.

Serve fish with rice, and pour gravy from stew over rice and fish. Be careful to remove clove of garlic and pepper pod before pouring gravy.

Greek-Fried Catfish

> 6 catfish fillets
> $^1/_2$ cup milk
> 1 egg
> 1 tsp. Greek seasoning
> 2 cups self-rising cornmeal
> 1 qt. peanut oil

Place catfish fillets in milk and egg mixture. Add Greek seasoning to cornmeal in brown paper bag. Shake well.

When ready to cook, drop pieces of catfish into bag of cornmeal and seasoning to cover fish completely. Use deep pot or skillet filled half

After adding peppers and celery, cook 15 minutes over very low heat. Add $^1/_2$ cup wine and mushrooms and cook 5 minutes. Add Worcestershire sauce, onion tops and sliced lemons. Let simmer and stir constantly. Use no water.

Season tenderloin catfish with Creole seasoning. Put a layer of sauce $^1/_2$ inch thick in bottom of Dutch oven, then a layer of fish, then a layer of sauce. Add another $^1/_2$ cup of wine. Do not stir. Cover tightly and let simmer 1 hour over very low heat. Do not stir, but do turn pot occasionally. Serve hot with crackers or rice. Serves six.

Pine Bark Stew

(This recipe was first named Pine Bark Stew because anglers in the South used pine bark to kindle a fire to cook their catch on the

full with cooking oil. Heat oil until just under smoking hot. Place several pieces of catfish into oil at same time so they will turn out golden brown and flaky. Cook on high until catfish fillets float to top. Drain well, and place on paper towels.

Catfish Croquettes

1 egg, well beaten
1 cup fish flakes
Creole seasoning
1/2 cup chopped green onion
    tops and parsley
2 1/2 cups boiled, mashed
    potatoes
2 T. flour
Oil for frying

Add egg, fish flakes, seasoning, onion tops and parsley to mashed potatoes. Mix thoroughly, and shape into balls. Roll balls in flour, and fry in oil until golden brown.

Catfish Parmesan

2 cups dry bread crumbs
3/4 cup Parmesan cheese
1/4 cup chopped parsley
1 tsp. paprika
1/2 tsp. leaf oregano
1/4 tsp. leaf basil
2 tsp. salt
1/2 tsp. pepper
6 skinned, filleted catfish
3/4 cup melted margarine
Lemon wedges

Combine bread crumbs, Parmesan cheese, parsley, paprika, oregano, basil, salt and pepper. Dip catfish in melted margarine, and roll in crumb mixture.

Arrange fish in well-greased oblong baking dish. Bake in 375°F oven 20 to 25 minutes, or until fish flakes easily when tested with fork. Garnish with lemon wedges.

Catfish Teriyaki

1 cup soy sauce
1/2 cup sugar
1/4 cup salad oil
2 tsp. grated fresh ginger
1 clove garlic, chopped
2 to 3 lbs. catfish fillets
1 T. sesame seed
Shredded lettuce (optional)

In bowl, combine soy sauce, sugar, oil, ginger and garlic. Let fillets stand in this mixture for several hours. Line shallow baking pan with aluminum foil. Lift fillets from soy sauce mixture. Arrange in pan.

Broil 5 to 7 inches from heat about 4 minutes, brushing once or twice with a little additional oil. Turn, brush with more oil, and sprinkle with sesame seeds. Broil 3 to 5 minutes longer or until fish flakes.

Serve on bed of shredded lettuce, if desired.

Catfish Hors d'Oeuvres

20 to 30 catfish fillets, cut into
    2-inch by 1-inch pieces
Salt
Soy-based steak sauce
Butter
Lemon juice
Bacon strips

Place fillets on platter. Lightly salt fillets and allow to sit about 30 minutes. Then sprinkle each piece of catfish with steak sauce. Apply a small pat of butter to each fillet. Sprinkle salt to taste. Squeeze freshly cut lemon over fillets, and cover fillets with strips of bacon.

This recipe can be cooked in smoker or in oven at 350°F for 30 to 40 minutes, until bacon is done.

Mustard Blackened Catfish

1 tsp. crushed yellow mustard
    seed
1 tsp. crushed brown mustard
    seed
1 tsp. ground mustard
1 tsp. dried thyme leaves
1/2 tsp. salt
1/4 tsp. coarse ground pepper
6 (about 8-10 oz. each) catfish
    fillets
1/4 cup melted butter
1 T. red wine vinegar
2 T. chopped fresh parsley

Combine the mustards, thyme, salt and pepper in pie pan. Dip catfish fillets in melted butter; coat with spice mixture. Heat a large cast-iron skillet over high heat until it is beyond the smoking stage and you see white ash in the skillet bottom, at least 10 minutes. Place fillets in hot pan; carefully spoon about 1 teaspoon melted butter on each fillet. Blacken, about 3 minutes until underneath is charred. Turn fish; spoon about 1 teaspoon melted butter on each fillet. Blacken, about 3 minutes or until fish flakes with fork. The time will vary according to the thickness of the fillet and the heat of the skillet. Repeat with remaining fillets. Remove from heat, keep warm. Sprinkle with vinegar and chopped parsley. Serves six.

**Mustard
Blackened Catfish**

**Catfish with Red
Beans and Rice**

Secrets of the Catfish Pros

Smoked Catfish

$1/2$ cup salt
$1/4$ cup dark brown sugar
1 gallon water
$1/2$ to $3/4$ lb. catfish, skin on
10 lbs. charcoal
1 lb. green hickory chunks

Prepare brine by mixing salt, brown sugar and water together. Soak whole, dressed catfish in brine 12 hours in refrigerator. Remove, rinse, and air-dry fish on rack 1 hour.

Prepare smoker. Use 5 pounds of charcoal first. Put hickory chunks on hot charcoal when fish are placed on smoker. Catfish should be 1 foot from heat. Smoke 4 hours. Check fire. Add additional charcoal and hickory if needed. Smoke another 2 to 4 hours. If you lift lid, add $1/2$ hour more cooking each time.

When finished, fish will be dark saffron color. Let fish cool before handling.

Smoked Catfish Dip

$3/4$ lb. smoked catfish
1 (8-oz.) pkg. soft, light cream cheese
2 T. lemon juice
$1/4$ tsp. garlic powder
2 T. milk

Flake fish and combine with cream cheese, lemon juice, garlic powder and milk. Makes 2 cups of dip and is delicious served with chips, crackers or raw vegetables.

Catfish with Red Beans and Rice

Beans and Rice
2 cups red beans
1 sweet onion, thinly sliced
3 cloves garlic, coarsely chopped
$1/2$ tsp. salt
$1/2$ tsp. pepper
2 cups converted white or brown rice
2 tsp. chopped fresh thyme leaves

Catfish
2 T. chile infused oil
6 (8-10 oz. each) catfish fillets
1 sweet onion, coarsely chopped
2 ripe tomatoes, coarsely chopped
2 tsp. chopped fresh thyme leaves
$1/4$ tsp. cayenne pepper

Prepare the beans and rice: prepare the red beans according to package directions; add the onion, garlic, salt and pepper. Meanwhile prepare the rice according to package directions; add the thyme leaves.

Make the catfish: heat 1 tablespoon oil in large skillet; place 3 fillets in pan with half of the onion. Sauté over medium-high heat, about 3 minutes on each side. Repeat with remaining fillets and onion. Place all fillets in pan; add tomatoes, thyme and pepper. Sauté, stirring occasionally, for 2 to 3 minutes or until fish flakes with fork.

To dine, present fish on bed of rice and beans. Sprinkle with cayenne pepper. Serves six.

Old-Time Catfish Stew

2 cups diced tomatoes
1 onion, chopped
1 small can whole kernel corn
1 cup water
2 garlic cloves, minced
Salt to taste
3 cups cubed potatoes
1 cup tomato juice
2 T. butter or margarine
$1/2$ tsp. freshly ground pepper
$1/4$ tsp. paprika
Sprinkling of dill
2 lbs. catfish fillets, cut into chunks

Combine all ingredients except catfish in a pot. Bring to a rolling boil, then reduce to simmering heat. Cook until the potatoes are tender. Add the catfish chunks and simmer 15 more minutes or until the fish begins to flake. Stir occasionally and serve piping hot. Serves four (ingredients can be doubled for a larger group).

Country Catfish Chowder

1 onion, diced
1 bell pepper, diced
$1/4$ lb. bacon, diced
1 ($10^3/4$-oz.) can cream of potato soup
1 (16-oz.) can whole kernel corn
3 potatoes, diced
1 (16-oz.) can diced carrots
2 lbs. catfish chunks
1 soup can whole milk
Salt to taste
Pepper to taste

Sauté onion and bell pepper with bacon until it is deep brown. Combine mixture with remaining ingredients in saucepan. Season with salt and pepper. Simmer for a half hour or until fish flakes with a fork and potatoes are done. Serves four.

Dilly Catfish and Lemon Butter

$1/2$ cup butter or margarine
2 T. lemon juice
2 lbs. catfish fillets
Fresh or dried dill weed

Melt butter in saucepan, stir in lemon juice. Pour mixture into baking dish. Place fillets in a single layer in pan. Sprinkle liberally with dill weed. Bake at 350°F until fish readily flakes. Serves four.

Tip: For an interesting alternative, substitute orange juice for lemon juice.

Grilled Catfish Fillets

½ cup cooking oil
¼ cup lemon juice
½ tsp. Tabasco sauce
Salt to taste
Pepper to taste
2 lbs. catfish fillets

Combine oil, juice, Tabasco, salt and pepper to make basting sauce. Place catfish fillets on grill a few inches above glowing coals. Baste thoroughly with sauce. Cook for 8 minutes, then turn and cook until fish readily flakes.

Tips: If desired, dust either dry dill or paprika on fillets. Leftover fillets can be reheated and covered with tartar sauce to make a tasty fish sandwich.

Catfish Dip

2 lbs. catfish fillets
3 T. salt
1 cup curd cottage cheese
1 (8-oz.) carton sour cream
½ cup shredded carrot
¼ cup chopped green onions
¼ cup chopped sweet pickles
   (or pickle relish)
1 T. chopped pimiento
1 T. horseradish
Parsley, chopped

Place fish in boiling water with 1 tablespoon of salt. Cook until fish flakes easily. Drain and set aside until cool. Flake and chill. Combine

remaining ingredients, except parsley, and mix well. Thoroughly stir in previously chilled fish. Garnish with parsley (or paprika can be substituted). Serve with raw celery, carrot sticks, chips or crackers. Makes four cups.

Campfire Catfish in Foil

1 catfish (1 lb. or less)
2 tsp. lemon or lime juice
2 T. butter or margarine
Salt to taste
Pepper to taste
Basil sprigs

Place fish in heavy-duty aluminum foil and drizzle citrus juice and butter on top. Sprinkle fish with salt and pepper. Place basil in body cavity and then fold foil to make a tight packet. Grill over coals of open fire (or on a grill) for 15 minutes. Flake with fork to make sure fish is done.

Tips: Place fresh vegetables in the packet with fish. If you like the taste of citrus, leave thin slices of lemon or lime in body cavity. Serves one.

Potato Catfish Patties

2 cups mashed potatoes
2 beaten egg yolks
½ cup minced onion
2 cups cooked, flaked catfish
¼ cup vegetable oil
Salt to taste
Pepper to taste
½ cup stone ground cornmeal

Combine all ingredients except cornmeal. Mix thoroughly and shape into small, flat patties. Roll in cornmeal until completely coated. Fry patties in skillet over medium heat until crisp and brown, turning only once.

Tip: For an interesting alternative, substitute rice for potatoes.

Pan-Fried Catfish

½ cup all-purpose flour
½ cup stone ground cornmeal
1 T. dried dill weed
Cayenne pepper to taste
¼ cup melted butter
2 T. oil
2 lbs. catfish fillets

Combine flour, cornmeal, dill weed and cayenne pepper in a dusting bag or shallow dish. Dip fillets in butter, then dredge or shake in dusting bag to coat. Fry in oil in nonstick skillet, turning once. Drain on paper towels. Serves four.

Catfish and Scallops with Mushrooms

1 cup cornmeal
Salt
Pepper
1 cup milk
1 egg
2-4 catfish fillets
¼ cup oil
Scallops
Mushrooms
½ tsp. basil
Beer
½ cup chicken broth

Combine cornmeal, salt and pepper. Mix milk and egg. Place fillets in milk mixture, then roll in cornmeal mixture. Heat oil in skillet. Cook each fillet 2-5 minutes per side. Brown scallops and mushrooms with basil. Add beer and chicken broth. Cook until mushrooms are done and liquid is evaporated.

Catfish and Scallops with Mushrooms

Grilled Catfish
Mexicana

Secrets of the Catfish Pros

Quick Cajun Catfish

¼ cup buttermilk
2 tsp. Dijon mustard
½ cup cornmeal
1 tsp. salt
1 tsp. paprika
1 tsp. onion powder
½ tsp. garlic powder
½ tsp. dried thyme leaves
½ tsp. ground red pepper
½ tsp. freshly ground black
    pepper
4 catfish fillets
4 lemon wedges

Lightly oil wire rack large enough to hold fillets in single layer. Place rack on baking sheet; set aside. In medium bowl, whisk together buttermilk and mustard until smooth. In shallow dish, combine cornmeal, salt, paprika, onion powder, garlic powder, thyme, ground red pepper and black pepper. Dip each fillet in buttermilk mixture, turning to coat. Transfer fillets to cornmeal mixture, turning to coat. Place fillets on prepared wire rack. Broil 4 inches from heat, until fish is opaque in center, about 3 minutes per side. Serve hot with lemon wedges.

Grilled Catfish Mexicana

½ cup milk
½ tsp. ground cumin
1½ lbs. catfish fillets, skin
    removed
2 T. olive oil
1 medium onion, finely
    chopped
½ cup chopped green, yellow
    or red pepper
¼ cup fresh snipped cilantro
    leaves
¼ tsp. salt
¼ tsp. freshly ground pepper
4 tsp. taco sauce or salsa
    (optional)
Lemon wedges
Lime wedges

Combine milk and cumin in large, plastic, zip top food-storage bag. Add fillets, turning to coat. Seal bag. Chill 1 hour. In 8-inch skillet, heat oil over medium heat. Reduce heat to low. Stir in onion, chopped pepper, cilantro, salt and pepper. Simmer, uncovered for 1-2 minutes, or until chopped pepper is tender-crisp. Set aside. Drain milk mixture from fillets; discard. Cut four 14 x 12-inch sheets of heavy-duty aluminum foil. Place 1 fillet on each sheet of foil. Top each fillet with one-fourth vegetable mixture and 1 teaspoon taco sauce. Fold long sides of foil together in locked folds. Fold and crimp short ends; seal tightly. Place foil packs on grill grate. Grill, covered for 11-17 minutes, or until fish is firm and opaque. Garnish with lemon and lime wedges.

Layered Spinach and Catfish Bake

1 T. olive oil
2 sweet onions, thinly sliced
2 cloves garlic, coarsely
    chopped
4 cups torn fresh spinach
    leaves
2 T. mayonnaise
2 tsp. red pepper flakes
½ tsp. salt
½ tsp. coarse ground pepper
4 (about 8-10 ounces each)
    catfish fillets
2 tsp. grated orange peel
Juice of 1 orange
2 T. chopped fresh mint leaves

Heat olive oil in skillet; add onions and garlic. Sauté over medium heat, stirring occasionally, about 7 minutes or until browned. Gradually add spinach leaves; continue sautéing about 3 minutes or until spinach is wilted. Stir in mayonnaise, red pepper flakes, salt and pepper. Place in bottom of 13 x 9-inch baking dish. Layer catfish fillets on spinach mixture; sprinkle with orange peel and juice of orange. Bake at 375°F for 15 to 20 minutes or until fish flakes with fork. Sprinkle with mint leaves.

Catfish Nuggets

1 egg, beaten
1 T. Worcestershire sauce
1 cup cornmeal
Catfish fillets
½ cup oil
2 T. butter
4 cloves garlic
White pepper
Lemon wedges

Combine egg and Worcestershire sauce. Place cornmeal in large, plastic zip top bag. Dip catfish in egg mixture, then place in cornmeal; shake to coat. Place catfish on waxpaper. Heat oil and butter in skillet. Add garlic, stir to blend. Add catfish; cook until fish flakes easily with a fork. Season with white pepper. Serve with lemon wedges.

Catfish and Fries

¼ tsp. salt
¼ tsp. black pepper
⅛ tsp. cayenne pepper
¼ tsp. thyme leaves
¾ cup flour
1½-2 lbs. catfish, cut into
    bite-size pieces
Oil
1-2 lbs. potatoes, cut into
    2½-inch sticks
¼ tsp. salt
2 tsp. lemon juice
2 T. butter, melted
Tomatoes
Onions
Soy sauce

Combine salt, black pepper, cayenne pepper, thyme and flour in a bag. Shake catfish fillets in bag. Heat oil in skillet. Fry fish until golden brown, 5-7 minutes. Fry potatoes in hot oil in nonstick skillet. Mix potatoes and fish on large platter. Sprinkle with salt, lemon juice and melted butter. Serve with sliced tomatoes and sliced onions sprinkled with soy sauce.

Tangy Orange Catfish

Marinade:
¼ cup orange juice
2 T. vegetable oil
2 T. soy sauce
1 T. lemon juice
1 tsp. minced garlic
⅛ tsp. pepper

Fish:
4 catfish fillets

Mix marinade ingredients in large, plastic, zip-top bag. Place fish fillets in bag. Seal and refrigerate for 3 hours, turning bag several times. Line broiler pan with foil. Coat broiler pan rack with nonstick spray, set rack in pan. Arrange fillets in single layer. Broil 4 inches from heat for 10 minutes, turning fish once.

Catfish Antipasto

4 (about 8-10 ounces each) catfish fillets
1 (6-oz.) jar marinated artichokes, reserve marinade
2 red peppers
2 medium zucchini or yellow squash
1 medium onion, cut into wedges
2 tsp. chopped fresh rosemary leaves
½ tsp. salt
½ tsp. coarse ground pepper

12 kalamata olives
12 cherry tomatoes

Prepare grill or wood fire: heat until coals are ash white or a wood fire has burned down to coals. Brush fillets with marinade from artichokes; place on oiled grate of grill. Place peppers, zucchini and onion around fillets. Brush vegetables with remaining marinade. Season with rosemary, salt and pepper. Grill over medium-hot coals, about 5 minutes on each side or until fish flakes with a fork.

To dine, serve at room temperature with marinated artichokes, olives and cherry tomatoes on bed of salad greens.

Catfish Fajitas

1 tsp. grated lime peel
¼ cup lime juice
2 T. olive oil
1 tsp. ground cumin
½ tsp. coarse ground pepper
¼ tsp. salt
⅛ tsp. cayenne pepper
4 (about 8-10 ounces each) catfish fillets
2 onions, cut into wedges
2 red peppers
1 poblano or pasilla chile pepper
2 jalapeño or serrano chile peppers
8 flour or corn tortillas
Guacamole
Sour cream

Prepare grill or wood fire: heat until coals are ash white or a wood fire has burned down to coals. Meanwhile, stir together lime peel, lime juice, olive oil, cumin, pepper, salt and cayenne pepper in small bowl. Place catfish in plastic food bag. Pour in marinade; seal tightly. Place

in 13 x 9-inch pan; let stand 10 to 15 minutes. Remove catfish from marinade; place on oiled grate of grill. Place onions and peppers around catfish. Grill catfish over medium-hot coals about 5 minutes on each side or until fish flakes with fork. Grill peppers about 6 minutes on each side or until charred. Place peppers in brown paper bag for 5 minutes to remove blackened skin. Cut peppers in half; remove seeds. Cut into strips. Grill tortillas about 2 minutes or until lightly toasted.

To dine, place onions and strips of peppers in bowl. Serve fish on grilled tortillas. Each person can make their own fajita by topping the fish with onions and peppers, guacamole and sour cream. Serve with lime wedges.

Crispy Oven-Fried Catfish

1 egg white
½ cup freshly squeezed lime juice
½ cup flour
½ cup white cornmeal
1 tsp. lemon pepper
½ tsp. cayenne pepper
¼ tsp. black pepper
1 T. coarsely chopped fresh dillweed
1½ tsp. dried basil
½ tsp. garlic powder
2 catfish fillets, halved
Lemon wedges
Dill sprig

Coat baking sheet with nonstick spray. In bowl, whisk together egg white and lime juice. Place flour in shallow dish. In separate bowl, combine cornmeal, peppers, dill, basil and garlic powder. Dip each fillet in flour, shake off excess. Then dip in egg white mixture, allowing excess to drip off. Roll each piece in cornmeal mixture. Place fillets on baking sheet; coat lightly with nonstick cooking spray. Bake 5 minutes, turn, bake another 5 minutes or until brown and crisp. Serve with lemon wedge and dill sprig garnish.

Rio Grande Blackened Catfish

½ tsp. red pepper
1 tsp. garlic salt
1 tsp. thyme
½ tsp. black pepper
½ lb. butter
Juice of 1 lemon
Catfish fillets, ½ inch thick,
    4-5 inches long
Fresh cilantro

Combine seasonings; mix well. Melt butter in skillet; set aside. Heat separate skillet as hot as possible. Stir lemon juice into melted butter skillet. Sprinkle fillets with seasoning mixture. Dip fillets in butter and drop in hot skillet. Cook 1-2 minutes, turn. There should be black crust on edge. If not, wait longer while the other side cooks. Serve with rice pilaf and tossed salad. Garnish with fresh cilantro.

Bullhead Marinated in Barbecue Sauce

3 T. chopped onions
1 T. olive oil
¼ cup packed brown sugar
¼ cup ketchup
¼ cup cider vinegar
2 T. Worcestershire sauce
½ tsp. dry mustard
¼ tsp. salt
¼ tsp. black pepper
⅛ tsp. dried oregano leaves

1½-2 lbs. bullheads, heads
    and skin removed

In small skillet, cook onions in olive oil over medium heat until onions are tender, about 3 minutes. Stir in brown sugar, ketchup, vinegar, Worcestershire sauce, dry mustard, salt, pepper and oregano. Cook, stirring occasionally, until mixture is bubbly. Reduce heat, simmer; stir occasionally for 10 minutes. Place bullheads in medium bowl. Pour marinade over fish. Cover, refrigerate for 30 minutes, turning fish at least once. Grease broiler pan. Remove fish from marinade with slotted spoon. Place on broiler pan. Broil at 550 degrees for 8 minutes. Baste with marinade; turn once. Broil 8 more minutes or until fish flakes easily.

Stovetop Catfish

1 can beer
2 cups crushed Stove Top
    stuffing
Oil
2 (1-lb.) catfish fillets

Leave beer open in refrigerator overnight. Combine stuffing and beer to make batter. Pour oil into skillet. Heat to medium. Dip catfish in batter; coat well. Fry fish in oil until fish is opaque and flakes easily with a fork.

Catfish Spicy Coating

2 cups Bisquick
1 tsp. garlic powder
1 T. paprika
1 T. chili powder
½ tsp. cayenne pepper
Salt
Pepper
2 eggs

1 T. water
Oil
Catfish fillets

Combine all dry ingredients. In a separate bowl, combine all wet ingredients. Dredge fillets in dry ingredients, then in wet ingredients, then back to dry ingredients. Heat oil in skillet. Fry fish in oil until golden brown.

Fried Bullhead

Bullheads, cleaned
Milk
¾ cup flour
½ cup cornmeal
2 tsp. paprika
½ tsp. ground black pepper
1 tsp. seasoned salt
Oil
Lemon or lime wedges

Clean bullheads, cover fillets with milk; refrigerate for 3 hours. Mix dry ingredients in plastic bag. Drain and dry fillets. Place fillets in bag; shake to coat fish evenly. Heat oil in skillet. Cook fillets 2-3 minutes per side until golden brown. Serve with lemon or lime wedges and tartar sauce.

INDEX